gorgeous cakes

Annie Bell was a chef before becoming a full-time food writer and author. She has written for *Vogue*, the *Independent*, and *Country Living*, and is now the principal cookery writer for *The Mail on Sunday*'s YOU magazine. Her books include *Evergreen*, which was shortlisted for the André Simon and Glenfiddich Food Writing awards; and more recently, *Soup Glorious Soup* and *The Camping Cookbook*. Annie is also the author of *Gorgeous Greens*, *Gorgeous Puddings*, *Gorgeous Suppers* and *Gorgeous Christmas*.

Annie Bell

gorgeouscakes

beautiful baking made easy

with photographs by Chris Alack

Vincent Square Books

This edition published in 2011 by
Vincent Square Books, an imprint of Kyle Books
23 Howland Street
London W1T 4AY
www.kylebooks.com

First published in Great Britain in 2005 by
Kyle Cathie Limited

ISBN 978-0-85783-038-8

A CIP catalogue record for this title is available from the British Library

Annie Bell is hereby identified as the author of this work in accordance with
Section 77 of the Copyright, Designs & Patents Act 1988.

Text copyright © 2005 by Annie Bell
Photographs copyright © 2005 by Chris Alack
Text layouts copyright © 2005 by Kyle Books

Copy editor: Stephanie Horner
Design: Mark Jonathan Latter
Indexer: Alex Corrin
Production: Sha Huxtable & Alice Holloway
YOU magazine: Angela Mason & John Koski
Colour reproduction: Colourscan Pty Limited
Printed in China by C&C Offset Printing Co., Ltd.

contents

introduction

Cakes we buy on the high street can never be as satisfying as the cakes in this book. And that's before we ever cut a slice. Baking cakes is the most basic experience of cooking that we share – weighing and beating ingredients together and licking out the mixing bowl – an innocent pleasure from childhood on. However much we rely on convenience food in everyday eating, we would still like to be able to bake well, perhaps because baking defines the idea of home for so many of us. Even those who never cook dinner will try their hand at a cake, and they should — it's a lovely, giving thing to do.

success made simple

Because doing it is the fun, I can't quite understand the instant cake mix industry, which plays on our lack of confidence. In the time it takes to read the instructions on the package and weigh out all the extras, you could make a cake from scratch from the essentials in your cupboard. Let me say: anybody can bake the cakes in this book. You don't need the latest mixer or a weekend at a patisserie masterclass. Choose your recipe, and get going. Now.

I can't say that a slice of cake is a necessary part of your diet, but of course that's the point of cakes – they're a luxury, an ornament to an occasion and even an occasion in themselves. Which might explain why tea parties, or tea outings somewhere posh, are so fashionable, and why cakes have lost their old frilly apron image and become glamorous. Besides, tea accommodates the smallest child and the most sophisticated adult at the same time. In this book you'll find cakes for all of them – and for every event from a soirée to a family gathering.

go for gorgeousness

To seize the mood of the moment, bake baroque. Borrow your colours and decorations from the worlds of fashion, design, showbiz and art and let rip. Think pink, yellow, and pale blue frostings, glitter, sprinkles, all the trimmings – and all in the best possible taste now that simple glazes have replaced the old thick stucco-type icing. You don't need a sugar toolkit because you can easily buy an array of edible bling and tubes of writing icing, no more difficult to use than a felt-tip pen, and more encouraging to the graffiti artist in you.

Sometimes, less is more. Most cakes never get consumed in anything so big as a slice. They get nibbled away, maybe after the icing has first been licked greedily from the top. A delicious morsel of cake is a generous reward for any task: I've catered to your personal portion control by including different-sized cakes and traybakes to cut up.

In this collection of recipes (a joint venture with YOU magazine), you'll recognise all your favourites, all-time greats and essentials – classic recipes for cupcakes, cheesecake, gooey chocolate cake, cakes for Christmas and Easter. I've got cakes without eggs, without flour, even without guilt. (Well, almost.)

There are cakes to share and to eat solo, sitting at the kitchen table. What would you serve to drink with cake? Could be a cup of tea, but a glass of pink champagne or a martini among girlfriends might be even better. You choose.

techniques and tips

While some of us swear by double sifting, adding wet and dry ingredients in a certain way, lining and flouring tins and so forth, there are few such rules in what follows. The recipes are as far as possible foolproof.

equipment

I rely heavily on my food processor and electric whisk – all the cakes can of course be made by hand but it's hard work! This aside, the most important aspect is the tin.

Because there are so many different shapes and sizes of cake tin, I have tried to hone down the list to a basic handful. Tins ideally should be non-stick, for ease of use as well as durability; tinplate tends to rust. And the more layers of non-stick the better – it's worth buying top of the range moulds that will last you. Some manufacturers are moving into flexible moulds, but I prefer the crusty base and sides that you achieve through the heat of the metal.

There is no need to have both sandwich and deep cake tins; shallow sponges can also be baked in deep tins. The most important feature is a removable base, which does away with the need to base-line cakes – always a fiddly job. Loaf tins are more complicated, some specified by length and others by the weight of the loaf they will bake. If in doubt the most accurate gauge is volume, measured by filling it with water. I would recommend the following sizes and ranges, which should cover you for the cakes in this book. I've also indicated three good stockists, together with the names of their baking tin ranges.

- (one or two) 20cm cake tin with a removeable base 9cm deep
- (one or two) 23cm cake tin with a removeable base 6cm deep
- 22cm (1.3l) loaf tin
- 30 x 23 x 4cm traybake or roaster
- 32 x 23cm Swiss roll tin or 36 x 25cm flat base oven tray
- (one or two) mini muffin tin
- (one or two) fairy-cake rack or deep bun tray
- (one or two) muffin rack or deep muffin tray
- one 23cm square cake tin, 23 x 23 x 4cm
  (or 30 x 19 x 4cm traybake or deep oblong oven tray)
- 23 x 3cm tart tin (loose-based are best).

For stockists of the 'Good Housekeeping' and 'Cook's Choice' ranges call Progress (01282 415511). For 'Blade' traybakes or roasters call Lakeland (015394 88100). Divertimenti (020 7935 0689) sells tart tins with 4cm sides in a variety of sizes.

cooking temperatures

I swear by fan ovens, which give consistently good results, especially if you're baking more than one cake or rack. In the recipes, I give temperatures for both fan and conventional ovens. Because ovens vary, I have allowed some leeway in the cooking times and, where necessary, give instructions for testing when your cake is done.

good ingredients

There are no hard-to-locate ingredients in my recipes. That said, cakes are virtuously simple creations, and the better the ingredients the tastier they will be. Unrefined sugar has far more flavour than refined. And you can have an organic field day with the butter, flour and eggs. In fact, if there's a chance that the bowl is likely to be licked out (which is half the point of baking), then it's wise to use organic eggs. From here it's about building in oodles of flavour – good vanilla extract, lemon zest, and a well-stocked liqueurs cabinet – while seasonal fresh fruit will bring any cake to life.

Jam I favour no-sugar varieties, such as St Dalfour, which are more alluring than they sound. Sweetened with concentrated fruit juice, they are that much more intensely flavoured than other jams, with a lovely loose set.

Chocolate There's no doubt that chocolate is tricky stuff to cook with – especially since the advent of dark chocolate containing anywhere between 45% and 85% cocoa solids, which in cooking terms are radically different ingredients. The latter will create havoc when certain ingredients or mixtures are introduced, causing it to seize up into a claggy lump. I prefer to play it safe with a lower percentage choc. The good news is that, whereas some years ago cooking chocolate was a derogatory term, today there's a wide selection of high-quality chocolate on the market designed for cooking. Look for cocoa butter in the list of ingredients – it has a profound effect on how the chocolate melts and combines with other ingredients. And texture is everything.

Dulce de leche This delicous caramel-like sauce has the consistency of the interior of a Rolo. Look in the baking section of good supermarkets – it's well worth seeking out.

Vanilla sugar Sachets of vanilla sugar are a staple on the Continent. To make your own, cut up a vanilla pod and whizz with 225g caster sugar in a food processor, then pass through a sieve. Store in a jar until required. If you use commercial vanilla sugar, however, mix it one part to three with ordinary caster sugar.

the art of decoration

Presentation is all and, if you're feeling creative, you may like to check out the following websites for cake-decorating supplies and equipment, including edible decorations:

• Jane Asher Party Cakes – www.jane-asher.co.uk
• Supercook – www.supercook.co.uk
• Squires Kitchen – www.squires-shop.com
• The Sugar Shack – www.sugarshack.co.uk

Food colouring I find the paste more effective than the liquid. (Supercook is widely available, and Bennett's comes in every shade of the rainbow. Also, silver and gold edible liquid colour is available from Divertimenti on 020 7935 0689.) For really pale pastel shades, I dip a skewer into the colouring then wave it through the icing until I get the right tint. A trickle of liquid or a small piece of paste can colour it too deeply.

say it with flowers

Fresh rose petals All cakes look magical with a handful of rose petals strewn over. Use just the small inner ones, and be sure they're organic or homegrown to avoid any pesticides. For how to make crystallised rose petals, see page 45.

Crystallised violets The ultimate pretty cake decoration; these are available from Comptoir Gascon in London and can be ordered on 020 7608 0851.

Flower waters I am as fond of rose and orange blossom water in cakes as I am of vanilla. They can be used in lieu of water to make an icing as well as an essence. And should you happen to have a local Middle Eastern deli, their flower waters are more fragrant than any other.

cupcakes and mini cakes

Cupcakes satisfy our inner five year old. They appeal to a childhood passion for the miniature, even when that child has long since grown up. More to the point, they give us permission to behave badly, hogging our individual treats to ourselves, nibbling the icing off the top before tasting the cake. (Remember those foil-wrapped deep cupcakes with more icing than crumb?) Their self-contained quality makes them a designer's dream for celebrations – hence the darlings of the fashion pack – and there is no birthday, minor or major, they can't decorate. Anyone with an eye for presentation can ice and stack them – perhaps as an edible message, letter by letter, or symbol by symbol; arranged with wit on a great tiered stand, they now substitute for the wedding cake that couples would rather not risk cutting.

Other miniatures have the same appeal. This chapter also includes iced choux puffs, and cute mouthfuls small enough to be served on a canapé tray with a martini (consider the Gin and Tonic Minis at cocktail hour). Appearance matters – pick a colourway, from pretty pastels to retro Fifties kitchen done in shades of buttercream to match the enamel. My selection should see all you addicts through every event.

You can use cupcakes just the way you would children's blocks and bricks – the messages can be coded in the design and layout instead of spelled out in icing.

child's play

oldie's birthday

Who's counting? When there are too many candles for the cake, just stick one in each cupcake, and arrange them on the table in the shape of the numerals for the age. If the guests are greedy, they'll never know how old you are.

wedding

Ain't no mountain high enough. Build one (or a skyscraper) of cupcakes – one per guest and a dozen or two spare. Each in white or silver icing, or perhaps sugar-flowered with pastel icing to match, on stands with real roses and cascading ribbons.

personalised cupcakes

Use tubes of writing icing to trace someone's initials or a special message – individual sweet graffiti.

kiddies

Keep the cupcakes tiny in proportion to their appetites – and then press into the icing all the bright sweeties they love – dolly mixtures, mini-marshmallows, fruit pastilles, the smallest jelly babies…

celebration minis

We gave up tiered cakes in favour of cupcakes to escape the old formalities. But now that you can buy paper cases in three sizes – mini-muffin, standard and muffin – you can produce miniature-tiered cakes. Slice off the tops of the two larger sizes to level them, coat first their sides and then their tops with butter icing, then stack them. One between two.

tips for success

For the best results set paper cases inside a bun, fairy-cake or muffin-tin rack. Failing this, put two cases inside each other. Cupcake or muffin? We say fairy cakes, cupcakes, sometimes buns. America does cupcakes, and also muffins. They do differ in shape, as the classic cupcake is narrower at the base and shallower than a big and boxy muffin (which is meant to mound out of its paper case: no peak, no muffin). It's a new world thing. The paper cases in three sizes are often labelled for muffins, likewise the tins. What matters more is to buy the right size of paper case.

Cupcakes are best eaten on the day they are made.

This is where it all began. If like me you had brothers and sisters, then probably the first vote you ever had, and lost, was whether it should be orange and lemon or chocolate cupcakes for tea. These had my vote, light fluffy miniatures with a sugary blanket of sticky lemon icing.

lemon cupcakes

Cake

110g unsalted butter, diced
110g golden caster sugar
Finely grated zest of 1 lemon
2 medium eggs, separated
75ml milk
140g plain flour
1 teaspoon baking powder
$1/4$ teaspoon sea salt

Icing

150g icing sugar, sifted
2 tablespoons fresh lemon juice, sieved
Yellow food colouring, paste or liquid
Sugared violets or other sugar flowers

Makes approx. 15

Preheat the oven to 170°C fan/190°C/gas mark 5. Cream the butter and sugar in a food processor until almost white. Incorporate the lemon zest and egg yolks, then the milk (it may look curdled at this point). Transfer the mixture to a large bowl. Sift the flour and baking powder twice, then fold them a third at a time into the butter mixture with the salt. Whisk the egg whites until stiff, then fold in two goes into the cake mixture, as lightly as possible. Arrange about 15 paper cases set inside two fairy-cake racks, and two-thirds fill with the cake mixture. Bake for 17–20 minutes until risen and springy to the touch. Remove and leave to cool.

Blend the icing sugar with the lemon juice, and tint it pale yellow with a little colouring. Smooth a heaped teaspoon of icing on each cake, but don't worry about completely covering. Decorate with sugared flowers. Leave to set for about 1 hour.

banoffee cupcakes

Cake

125g unsalted butter, diced

125g golden caster sugar

3 medium eggs

3 tablespoons milk

250g self-raising flour

1 teaspoon baking powder

1 heaped teaspoon ground cinnamon

3 ripe bananas, mashed

Topping

350g (approx.) dulce de leche
(see page 9)

Chocolate hearts and icing sugar
to decorate

Makes 24

Preheat the oven to 170°C fan/190°C/gas mark 5 and arrange 24 paper cases inside two fairy-cake or bun racks. Cream the butter and sugar together, then incorporate the eggs, one at a time, and then the milk. Don't worry about the mixture appearing curdled at this point. Sift and add the dry ingredients, then stir in the mashed bananas. You can prepare the mixture in a food processor, in which case give it just a quick whizz after adding the bananas. Fill the paper cases two-thirds full, with about a tablespoon of mixture, and bake for 25 minutes until risen and golden. Leave to cool.

Smooth a teaspoon of dulce de leche over the surface of each cake, but don't worry about completely covering it, then decorate with a chocolate heart in the centre. If you like, dust with icing sugar using a tea strainer.

With a flavour that merits a tome to itself, these are deeply, darkly chocolatey, a little more bitter than usual, with an icing that is pure chocolate truffle.

truffle cupcakes

Preheat the oven to 180°C fan/200°C/gas mark 6. Pour 100ml boiling water over the cocoa in a small bowl and whisk until smooth, then cool to room temperature. Cream the butter and sugar in a food processor until pale. Incorporate the egg, then the dry ingredients and finally the cocoa solution. Arrange about 14 paper cases inside two fairy-cake racks and half fill them with the mixture. Bake the cakes for 17–20 minutes until risen and springy to the touch, then remove and leave to cool.

Bring the cream to the boil in a small saucepan and pour over the dark chocolate in a small bowl. Leave for a few minutes, then stir to dissolve the chocolate. Leave it a few minutes longer and then stir again – you should have a thick glossy cream. If the chocolate doesn't completely melt, transfer the mixture to a bowl set over a pan of simmering water and heat it a little, stirring until it is smooth.

Drop 1 teaspoon of the icing onto each cake and spread it towards the edge using a small palette knife, or unserrated table knife. Scatter over some chocolate curls, dust with icing sugar, if you like, using a tea strainer, and set aside for about 1 hour to set.

sweetie counter

• Crown with a Malteser or mini Rolo instead of the curls.

Cake

25g cocoa powder

50g unsalted butter, diced

100g golden caster sugar

1 medium egg

85g plain flour

1/2 teaspoon bicarbonate of soda

1/4 teaspoon baking powder

Icing

100ml double cream

100g dark chocolate (about 75% cocoa solids), broken into pieces

Mini chocolate curls (dark or milk)

Icing sugar for dusting (optional)

Makes approx. 14

Very Wisteria Lane... pound-cake sponge slathered with vanilla butter icing dyed a sunny pastel shade to match the enamelware.

vanilla cupcakes

Cake

110g unsalted butter, diced
110g golden caster sugar
110g plain flour
2 medium eggs
1 teaspoon baking powder

Icing

100g icing sugar, sifted
150g unsalted butter, softened
$^1/_2$ teaspoon vanilla extract
Blue food colouring, paste
   or liquid
Dolly mixtures

Makes approx. 15

Preheat the oven to 180°C fan/200°C/gas mark 6. Place all the ingredients for the cake in a food processor and cream together. Arrange about 15 paper cases inside two fairy-cake racks and two-thirds fill them with the cake mixture. Bake for 17–20 minutes until risen and springy to the touch, then remove and leave to cool.

To make the butter icing, place the icing sugar with the butter, vanilla extract and a little food colouring in a food processor and cream until light and fluffy. Using a small palette knife or unserrated table knife, trowel this over the surface of the cakes, then decorate with about 3 dolly mixtures apiece.

retro

• Colour the icing a bright pastel shade of green, or dusky orange with red and yellow colouring, or pink.

A cream cake in miniature, with all the charm of a cappuccino: the coffee-flavoured froth and the sprinkling of chocolate that is the main reason for ordering one.

cappuccino cupcakes

Cake

1 heaped tablespoon
  cocoa powder

110g plain flour

110g golden caster sugar

110g unsalted butter, diced

2 medium eggs

1 teaspoon baking powder

Topping

200ml double cream

3 tablespoons strong
  black coffee

30g icing sugar

Chocolate powder

Chocolate covered coffee
  beans or buttons

Makes approx. 14

Preheat the oven to 180°C fan/200°C/gas mark 6. Blend the cocoa with 2 tablespoons boiling water in a small bowl and leave to cool to room temperature. Place all the ingredients for the cake, including the cooled cocoa paste, in a food processor and cream together. Put about 14 paper cases inside two fairy-cake racks and two-thirds fill them with the cake mixture. Bake for 17–20 minutes until risen and springy to the touch, then remove and leave to cool.

To make the topping, whisk the cream, coffee and icing sugar until stiff. Drop a teaspoon of the cream onto each cake, dust with chocolate powder using a tea strainer, and add a bean or button. Set aside in a cool place until ready to serve.

theme on cream

• Replace the coffee cream with whipped cream and scatter over M&Ms or 100s and 1000s.

• Stick a splinter or two of chocolate flake in the top like an ice-cream.

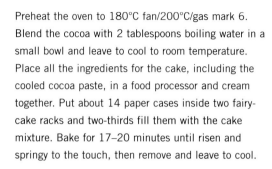

white chocolate butterfly cakes

Preheat the oven to 170°C fan/190°C/gas mark 5. Cream the butter and sugar in a food processor until almost white. Incorporate the orange zest and egg yolks, then the milk and continue beating until homogenised. Transfer the mixture to a large bowl. Sift the dry ingredients twice, then fold them a third at a time into the butter mixture. Whisk the egg whites until stiff, then fold in two goes into the cake mixture, as lightly as possible. Fill 20–24 paper cases, set inside two fairy-cake racks, about half full with the cake mixture, and bake for 20 minutes (the lower rack may take a few minutes longer). Remove and leave them to cool in the racks.

To make the topping, spoon the mascarpone into a bowl and beat in the vanilla extract, then the syrup and icing sugar. Place the chocolate in a bowl set over simmering water in a small saucepan and gently melt it. Using a small, sharp knife, cut out a shallow cone from the centre of each cake and halve it. Fill the cavities with the vanilla cream. Shake some 100s and 1000s into a small bowl.

Dip the curved tips of the butterfly wings first into the melted chocolate and then into 100s and 1000s. Set them into the vanilla cream at an angle, tips uppermost. Set aside in a cool place. If keeping for longer than a few hours, store in an airtight container.

Cake

175g unsalted butter, diced
175g golden caster sugar
Finely grated zest of 1 orange
2 large eggs, separated
100ml milk
175g plain flour
1$^1/_2$ teaspoons baking powder

Topping

250g mascarpone
1 teaspoon vanilla extract
25g golden syrup
10g icing sugar, sifted
50g white chocolate, broken up
100s and 1000s

Makes approx. 20–24

pistachio and white chocolate buns

Cake

110g unsalted butter, diced

110g golden caster sugar

Finely grated zest of 1 orange

2 medium eggs, separated

75ml milk

140g plain flour

1 teaspoon baking powder

$1/4$ teaspoon sea salt

25g shelled raw pistachio nuts, coarsely chopped

25g white chocolate chips

Topping

1 tablespoon shelled raw pistachio nuts

75g apricot jam

Makes 12-14

Preheat the oven to 170°C fan/190°C/gas mark 5. Cream the butter and sugar in a food processor until almost white. Incorporate the orange zest and egg yolks, then the milk and beat until homogenised. Transfer the mixture to a large bowl. Sift the flour and baking powder twice together, then fold them in two goes into the butter mixture, then add the salt, the 25g pistachios and chocolate chips.

Whisk the egg whites until stiff, then fold in two goes into the cake mixture, as lightly as possible. Fill 12–14 paper cakes, set inside one or two fairy-cake racks, two-thirds full with the cake mixture and bake for 15–20 minutes (the lower rack may take a few minutes longer). Remove and leave to cool in the racks.

Place the pistachios in a coffee grinder and finely chop. Gently warm the jam in a small pan until it thins, then pass it through a sieve.

Brush the cakes with the jam and scatter with ground pistachios.

As refined as their name implies: a honey-scented sponge, nip of sherry in the icing and the Edwardian touch of pink and white rose petals. Perfect for your own garden party. If you happen to have any of those pretty scallop-shaped moulds, this would be a good outing for them.

red, white and blue buns

Cake

2 large eggs

25g golden caster sugar

Finely grated zest of 1 lemon

2 tablespoons runny honey

50g plain flour

1 teaspoon baking powder

Pinch of sea salt

50g ground almonds

125g unsalted butter, melted and cooled, plus a little for greasing

Icing

200g icing sugar, sifted

2 tablespoons dry sherry

Blue food colouring, paste or liquid

Red and white rose petals* for decorating, or sugar flowers

Makes 15

Whisk the eggs and sugar together until almost white. Add the lemon zest and honey. Sift the flour and baking powder twice together and then lightly fold into the egg mixture with the salt and ground almonds. Take care not to overwork it. Gently fold the cooled, melted butter into the egg and almond mixture.

Chill the mixture in the fridge for 30 minutes. Meanwhile preheat the oven to 190°C fan/210°C/gas mark 6^1/$_2$. Brush the inside of two fairy-cake racks with a little melted butter. Spoon the mixture into the prepared racks, filling each one two-thirds full. Bake the buns in the oven for 9-10 minutes until golden. Run a knife around the edge of the buns then turn them out onto a wire rack to cool.

When barely cool, blend the icing sugar with the sherry in a bowl and tint it a pale turquoise. Smooth a little icing over the surface of each cake using a small palette knife or an unserrated table knife, and scatter over a few rose petals or sugar flowers. Leave to set for about 1 hour and eat as soon as possible.

* If the roses come from your garden you may be able to vouch for their purity, otherwise try to buy them from an organic outlet.

Complete with ice and a slice in the form of mini-marshmallows and jellied lemon sweeties, these are small, sweet and boozy. In fact, the perfect attendants to vodka shots and martinis, when you're in the mood for cake and wine – one of life's more decadent partnerships.

gin and tonic minis

Cake

2 medium egg whites
Pinch of sea salt
$1/4$ teaspoon cream of tartar
60g icing sugar, sifted
35g plain white flour, sifted
$1^1/2$ tablespoons tonic water

Topping

125g mascarpone
1 tablespoon gin
2 teaspoons golden syrup
Green food colouring, paste or liquid
Mini jellied lemon slices
Mini white marshmallows

Makes approx. 20

Preheat the oven to 150°C fan/170°C/gas mark 3. Whisk the egg whites in a large bowl with the salt and cream of tartar until they are risen (I use a hand-held electric whisk for this). Now whisk in the sugar, a couple of tablespoons at a time, sprinkling it over the egg whites and whisking for about 20 seconds with each addition. Fold the sifted flour into the meringue in three goes, and then stir in the tonic water. Arrange 20 mini-muffin paper cases inside two mini-muffin racks, and two-thirds fill with the mixture using a teaspoon. Bake the cakes for 10-15 minutes until lightly golden on the surface and springy to the touch. Remove and leave to cool.

To prepare the topping, spoon the mascarpone into a bowl and beat in the gin, and then the syrup, and tint it the palest green with a little of the colouring. Spread a little of the icing over the surface of each cake using a small palette knife or unserrated table knife, and spear with a jellied lemon slice and mini-marshmallow on a cocktail stick. Set aside in a cool place until ready to serve.

cocktail minis

• Replace the gin with malibu.
• Replace the gin with advocaat and tint the icing a pale orange with red and yellow colouring, and top with a jellied orange slice.

Miniature eclairs, filled with orange custard, and a sticky orange icing. If these are destined for adults then grand marnier is too tasty to pass up, but if they're for children, use orange juice instead.

orange sugar puffs

Custard

4 large egg yolks

80g icing sugar, sifted

50g plain flour, sifted

425ml full-fat milk

2 strips of orange peel

1 tablespoon grand marnier or cointreau (optional)

Puffs

50g unsalted butter

Pinch each of sea salt and caster sugar

75g plain flour, sifted

3 medium eggs

Icing

100g icing sugar, sifted

1 tablespoon grand marnier or cointreau, or fresh orange juice, sieved

Orange or yellow food colouring, paste or liquid

Sugar flowers to decorate

Makes approx. 20

To make the custard, whisk the egg yolks and icing sugar together in a non-stick saucepan until smooth. Whisk in the flour in two goes to make a thick creamy paste. Bring the milk to the boil in a small pan with the orange peel, and whisk it gradually into the egg mixture. Return the pan to a low heat, cook for a few minutes until the custard thickens, stirring vigorously with a wooden spoon or whisk to disperse any lumps that form. The custard should not boil, but the odd bubble indicates it is hot enough to thicken properly. Cook for a few more minutes, stirring constantly. Pour the custard into a bowl, discard the peel, stir in the grand marnier, if using, cover the surface with clingfilm and leave to cool.

Preheat the oven to 200°C fan/220°C/gas mark 7. To make the puffs, put the butter, salt and sugar in a small pan with 200ml water and bring to the boil. Stir in the flour off the heat and beat the dough with a wooden spoon until smooth. Return the pan to a medium-high heat and cook for a couple of minutes, stirring constantly. Allow to cool for about 5 minutes, then beat in the eggs, one at a time.

Butter and flour 1–2 baking sheets, and place heaped teaspoons of dough about 5cm apart. Bake for 10 minutes, then reduce the heat to 160°C fan/180°C/gas mark 4 and bake for 20 minutes until golden. Slice off the tops to prevent the puffs from being soggy, scoop out and discard any uncooked inside. Cool on a wire rack.

Fill the puffs with custard and replace the lids. Blend the icing sugar with the grand marnier or orange juice, adding just enough water to make a thick trickling consistency. Tint it pale orange with a little colouring. Spread about $1/2$ teaspoon icing over each puff and let it trickle down, then decorate with sugared flowers. Leave in a cool place for about 1 hour. They are best eaten the day they are made.

Crème de menthe frappé is an acquired taste, but a bottle of the stuff in the wine rack has all sorts of culinary uses, including tinting icing the palest eau-de-nil with a hint of mint.

angel mint cakes

Cake

8 medium egg whites, at
   room temperature
$^1/_4$ teaspoon sea salt
1 teaspoon cream of tartar
250g icing sugar, sifted
140g plain flour, sifted

Topping

500g mascarpone
4 tablespoons crème de menthe
40g golden syrup
25g mini white marshmallows

Makes approx. 35 squares

Preheat the oven to 150°C fan/170°C/gas mark 3. Butter and line the base of a 30 x 23 x 4cm baking tin with baking paper. Whisk the egg whites in a large bowl with the salt and cream of tartar until they are risen (I use a hand-held electric whisk for this). Now whisk in the sugar, a couple of tablespoons at a time, sprinkling it over the egg whites and whisking for about 20 seconds with each addition. Fold the sifted flour into the meringue in three goes, then transfer the mixture to the prepared baking tin and smooth the surface. Bake the sponge for 30 minutes until lightly golden on the surface and springy to the touch. Run a knife around the edge of the tin, turn the cake out onto a board and leave it paper-side down to cool.

To prepare the topping, spoon the mascarpone into a bowl and beat in the crème de menthe, and then the syrup. Remove the paper from the base of the cake, slit it in half using a bread knife, and spread the lower half with half the mascarpone using a palette knife. Sandwich with the top half and smooth over the remaining topping. Trim off the edges of the cake and slice into 3–4cm squares – again, a bread knife is best for this. Scatter the marshmallows over the squares and gently press into the icing, then transfer to serving plates.

Cocktails wouldn't be cocktails without the occasional cherry, but rather on a cake than in the glass. In truth, though, these are just as good without. Try them with a champagne cocktail or a 'sticky' – a glass of sweet wine.

coconut cubes

Cake
225g unsalted butter, diced
225g golden caster sugar
3 medium eggs
150ml milk
225g self-raising flour, sifted
1^1/$_2$ teaspoons baking powder, sifted
Finely grated zest of 1 lemon

Topping
100g raspberry jam
75g shredded or desiccated coconut
75g undyed glacé cherries, halved
  (optional)

Makes approx. 35 squares

Preheat the oven to 170°C fan/190°C/gas mark 5. Butter a 30 x 23 x 4cm baking tin. Place the butter and caster sugar in a food processor and beat together until pale and fluffy. Incorporate the eggs one at a time, scraping down the sides of the bowl if necessary, then add the milk and whizz until creamy. Gradually add the flour and baking powder through the funnel with the motor running, then incorporate the lemon zest. Transfer the mixture to the prepared baking tin and smooth the surface. Bake for 30 minutes until golden and shrinking slightly from the sides, and a skewer comes out clean from the centre. Run a knife around the edge of the tin and leave the cake to cool.

To prepare the topping, warm the raspberry jam over a gentle heat in a small saucepan until it thins, then pass through a sieve. Brush the surface of the cake with the jam and scatter over the coconut. Shake the tin from side to side to evenly coat the surface and tip out the excess coconut. Remove the cake from the tin, trim off the edges and cut it into 3–4cm squares and decorate each cube with half a glacé cherry, cut-side down. Transfer to serving plates.

good
old-fashioned
cakes

Hello old friends – here are classic comfort cakes, family favourites and nursery treats from the traditional baking repertoire we grew up with. My own memories of home come back when I cut a slice of personal past: a Victoria sponge spread with strawberry jam *is* the taste of my mother's cooking. Although it was hardly exclusive to our family – it has been the national standard since its name was borrowed from Queen Victoria, and it shares its basic mix (equal quantities of butter, sugar, eggs and flour) with the American pound cake and the French *quatre quarts*. Once you know how to put it together, then the rest of the cake universe opens before you for just a little effort in icing and filling.

Certain flavours stir up deep memories for me: lemon cake always does it – and sticky ginger and apple. What I don't like so much is a filling of too-sweet buttercream – here I set tradition aside and use mascarpone, which needs only whisking with jam, lemon curd or chocolate spread to become a luxurious interior. Or you could compromise with the French buttercream on page 158, two-thirds proper custard to one-third butter, the perfect ratio, or try the whisked white chocolate buttercream on page 35.

The one that takes me back – lazy summer days, sitting on the lawn
making daisy chains and shelling peas.

classic victoria sponge cake

Cake

225g unsalted butter, diced

225g golden caster sugar

225g self-raising flour

2 teaspoons baking powder

4 medium eggs

100ml milk

Filling

150g strawberry jam

180ml double cream (for the
rich version)

Icing sugar for dusting

Makes 1 x 20cm cake

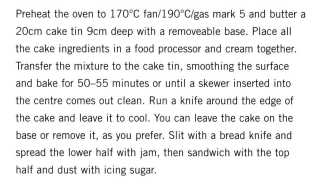

Preheat the oven to 170°C fan/190°C/gas mark 5 and butter a
20cm cake tin 9cm deep with a removeable base. Place all
the cake ingredients in a food processor and cream together.
Transfer the mixture to the cake tin, smoothing the surface
and bake for 50–55 minutes or until a skewer inserted into
the centre comes out clean. Run a knife around the edge of
the cake and leave it to cool. You can leave the cake on the
base or remove it, as you prefer. Slit with a bread knife and
spread the lower half with jam, then sandwich with the top
half and dust with icing sugar.

the rich version

The cake is instantly whisked into the realms of luxury if you
spread 180ml whipped double cream on top of the jam before
sandwiching it. Take care not to overwhisk the cream however,
stopping just as it starts to form soft peaks.

thoroughly modern fillings

whisked white chocolate buttercream

115g white chocolate, broken into pieces
115g unsalted butter

Makes enough to fill 1 x 20cm cake

Gently melt the chocolate in a bowl over a pan of simmering water, then cool to room temperature. Cream the butter, add the melted chocolate and combine. Whisk with an electric whisk for 1–2 minutes until mousse-like and almost white.

Mascarpone replaces butter icing as the new darling on the block – the perfect consistency to fill a cake. Combine it with jam, spread or syrup that suits the sponge, or try these:

espresso cream

A delicious filling for coffee, chocolate and nut cakes.

250g mascarpone
1 tablespoon espresso, or very strong instant coffee, cooled
25g golden syrup
10g icing sugar, sifted

Makes enough to fill 1 x 20cm cake or 1 x 22cm loaf

Spoon the mascarpone into a bowl and beat in the coffee, then the syrup and icing sugar. Cover and chill until required.

mascarpone and lemon curd cream

A good filling for orange and lemon cakes, ones containing fruit, or simply a plain sponge.

100g lemon curd (see page 36)
250g mascarpone

Makes enough to fill 1 x 20cm cake

Blend the lemon curd and mascarpone together in a bowl. Cover and chill until required.

butterscotch cream

Good with chocolate, coffee, spice cakes and nut sponges.

250g mascarpone
1 teaspoon treacle
20g icing sugar, sifted
Knife tip of ground cinnamon

Makes enough to fill 1 x 20cm cake

Blend all the ingredients together in a bowl. Cover and chill until required.

A lemon lover's dream, every bit as intense as a French lemon tart. For a lighter version, fill with lemon curd to within 1cm of the rim and dust the top with icing sugar. Cover and set the cake aside for a few hours to let the curd settle into the crumb.

rich lemon curd sponge

Cake
225g unsalted butter, diced
225g golden granulated sugar
225g self-raising flour
2 teaspoons baking powder
4 medium eggs
50ml double cream
Finely grated zest and juice of 1 lemon
2 tablespoons dark rum (optional)

Filling
Finely grated zest and juice of 1 lemon
2 medium organic eggs
60g unsalted butter
90g golden granulated sugar
200g mascarpone

Topping
Juice of 1 lemon
50g golden granulated sugar

Makes 1 x 20cm cake

First make the lemon curd for the filling. Place all the ingredients except the mascarpone in a bowl set over a saucepan of simmering water. Whisk until the butter melts, then continue to whisk for a couple of minutes until the mixture resembles a thick custard. Pass it through a sieve into a bowl, cover with clingfilm and chill for a couple of hours until it sets.

Preheat the oven to 170°C fan/190°C/gas mark 5 and butter a 20cm cake tin 9cm deep with a removeable base. Place all the cake ingredients in a food processor and cream together. Transfer the mixture to the cake tin, smooth the surface and bake for 50–55 minutes or until a skewer inserted into the centre comes out clean. Run a knife around the edge of the cake. Combine the lemon juice and sugar in a bowl, stirring to evenly distribute it, then spoon over the top of the cake. Leave it to cool, allowing the juice to sink into the sponge.

Blend 100g of the lemon curd with the mascarpone. (You won't need all of the lemon curd but the rest will keep well in the fridge for a week and is delicious on toast or bread.) You can leave the cake on the base or remove it as you prefer. Slit with a bread knife and spread the lower half with the lemon mascarpone cream, then sandwich with the top half.

If not serving within a few hours, cover and chill the cake. Bring it back up to room temperature 30–60 minutes before serving.

This has always been an effortlessly pretty cake, especially when it's iced in this way with dark and white chocolate drizzled over. It can also be made as a round 20cm cake, baked for 40 minutes. In this case you can slit and fill it with the Espresso or Butterscotch Cream on page 35.

marble cake

Preheat the oven to 170°C fan/190°C/gas mark 5 and butter a 23cm ring mould. Place the dark chocolate in a bowl set over a pan with a little simmering water in it and gently melt, then leave it to cool.

Cream the butter and sugar together, either in a food processor or by hand. Beat in the eggs one at a time, then the milk. Don't worry if the mixture appears curdled at this point; it will cream again in the next stage. Sift together the flour and baking powder and gradually whisk them into the mixture.

Remove half the mixture to another bowl and stir in the cooled, melted chocolate and chocolate chips. Stir the vanilla into the other half. Drop alternate dessertspoons of the mixture into the prepared tin – you should have two layers. Smooth the surface with a spoon and bake for 30–35 minutes or until golden and risen, and a skewer inserted into the centre comes out clean. Remove the cake from the oven, run a knife around the inner and outer edges of the tin, turn the cake onto a wire rack and leave it to cool.

If the cake has risen unevenly, trim the bottom a little to even it out. To ice the cake, melt the white and dark chocolate separately in bowls set over pans of simmering water. Using a teaspoon, drizzle first the white chocolate and then the dark chocolate over the cake – imagine you are Jackson Pollock for this bit. Leave the chocolate to set for a couple of hours. The cake will be good for several days, very crumbly to begin with, but it will firm up on the second day.

Cake

100g dark chocolate (about 50% cocoa solids), broken into pieces
110g unsalted butter, diced
150g golden caster sugar
2 medium eggs
75ml milk
200g self-raising flour
1 teaspoon baking powder
25g dark chocolate chips
$1/2$ teaspoon vanilla extract

Icing

40g white chocolate, broken into pieces
40g dark chocolate, broken into pieces

Makes 1 x 23cm ring

Sue Lawrence is the Scottish queen of baking and excels in gingerbreads. This one, from her *Book of Baking*, is wonderfully sticky and filled with rhubarb fool. Play up its pretty-in-pink hue to make a Valentine's Day offering. Cut out a heart shape from a 7cm square of card. Whizz 1 tablespoon icing sugar with a few drops of pink or red food colouring in a coffee grinder and use a tea strainer to sift the sugar through the heart template.

all spiced up

Cake

150ml light beer or lager
175g dark muscovado sugar
$1/2$ teaspoon bicarbonate of soda
200g self-raising flour
2 teaspoons ground ginger
2 large eggs
100g golden caster sugar
125ml sunflower oil

Rhubarb fool

500g young rhubarb, trimmed and sliced
1 tablespoon elderflower syrup
60g golden caster sugar
225ml whipping cream

Makes 6 squares

Place the beer and 125g of the muscovado sugar in a small saucepan and slowly bring to the boil, working out any lumps in the sugar with the back of a spoon. Remove from the heat and stir in the bicarbonate of soda. Leave to cool for about 1 hour.

Preheat the oven to 160°C fan/180°C/gas mark 4, and butter and line a 23 x 30 x 4cm traybake tin. Sift the flour and ginger into a bowl. Whisk together the eggs, remaining muscovado sugar, caster sugar and oil, then slowly add this to the flour, stirring. Add the beer mixture in two goes, gently mixing it in. Tip into the prepared tin and bake for 25–30 minutes or until just firm to the touch. Run a knife around the edge of the cake and cool in the tin for 30 minutes, then turn out onto a wire rack to cool, surface uppermost. Peel off the paper when cold.

To make the fool, place the rhubarb in a pan with the elderflower syrup and sugar and bring slowly to the boil, then cover and cook over a low heat for 8–10 minutes until just tender, stirring halfway through. Drain the rhubarb into a sieve and leave to cool over the pan. Whip the cream until stiff, then fold in the cooled rhubarb.

If the cake has risen unevenly, trim the bottom a little to even it. Slit the cake in half widthways, spread the fool over one half, then sandwich with the other. Cut into 6 squares, each about 7cm. The filled squares are best eaten the day they are made, but the cake itself can be made several days in advance and will stand in as a stock recipe without the fool.

upside-down apricot cake

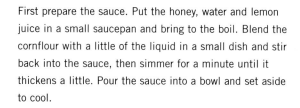

Sauce
100g set honey
100ml water
Juice of 1/2 lemon
1 teaspoon cornflour

Apricots
30g light muscovado sugar
30g salted butter
5 apricots, halved
  and stoned

Cake
150g salted butter
150g golden caster sugar
2 medium eggs
Finely grated zest of 1 lemon
125ml milk
200g plain flour, sifted
1 1/2 teaspoons baking
  powder, sifted

Makes 1 x 20cm cake

First prepare the sauce. Put the honey, water and lemon juice in a small saucepan and bring to the boil. Blend the cornflour with a little of the liquid in a small dish and stir back into the sauce, then simmer for a minute until it thickens a little. Pour the sauce into a bowl and set aside to cool.

Preheat the oven to 180°C fan/200°C/gas mark 6. Cream together the light muscovado sugar and 30g salted butter and, using your fingers, smear it over the base of a 20cm cake tin 9cm deep with a removeable base. Place the apricots cut-side down on top of the butter and sugar mixture.

To make the cake, cream the butter and sugar in a food processor until light and fluffy. Add the eggs, one at a time, and then the lemon zest. Incorporate the milk, the flour and baking powder.

Spoon the mixture on top of the apricots, smoothing the surface and bake for 45–50 minutes until the top is golden and a skewer inserted into the centre comes out clean.

Run a knife around the edge and leave the cake to cool for about 15 minutes. Place a plate on top of the cake tin and invert it, pressing the base down until the cake touches the plate. Now carefully run a knife between the base of the tin and the cake and lift it off. The cake can be served hot or at room temperature, though it's best eaten the same day. Just before serving pour the honey sauce over the surface, allowing it to trickle over the sides.

Lemon cakes offer the opportunity of a sharp, sassy icing, as the juice can be used in lieu of water to mouth-watering effect. You don't have to use food colouring, but there is something about primrose yellow icing. The roses, too, are a frill – ideally use ones from your garden, and if you're buying them try to ensure they're organic and unsprayed.

iced lemon loaf with crystallised rose petals

Crystallised rose petals

1 red and 1 white rose
1 egg white
Caster sugar for dusting

Cake

4 medium eggs
200g caster sugar
Finely grated zest of 1 lemon
100ml double cream
200g plain white flour
1 heaped teaspoon baking powder
65g unsalted butter, melted and cooled
4 tablespoons lemon juice

Icing

150g icing sugar, sifted
2 tablespoons lemon juice
Yellow food colouring, paste
    or liquid (optional)

Makes 1 x 22cm loaf

You need to prepare the petals well in advance. A fan oven with a defrost setting that allows you to use the fan without heat is ideal for drying them. Otherwise, pick a warm and draughty spot. Carefully pull the petals off the stalks. Lay them on a worktop, and very lightly paint the top with egg white. Sift over an even layer of sugar until they appear frosted. Repeat on the other side. Lay them on a wire rack and leave to dry for several hours, until they are brittle and crisp.

Preheat the oven to 170°C fan/190°C/gas mark 5. Brush the inside of a 22cm (1.3l) loaf tin with melted butter. Unless your tin is non-stick, line the base with baking paper. Whisk the eggs, sugar and lemon zest together, then add the cream. Sift the flour and baking powder together and fold in gradually. Stir in the melted butter and 3 tablespoons of the lemon juice. Pour the mixture into the cake tin and bake for 40–50 minutes until golden and risen and a skewer inserted into the centre comes out clean. Run a knife around the edge of the tin, turn the cake onto a wire rack, remove the paper then stand it the right way up. Sprinkle with the remaining lemon juice and leave to cool.

Place the cake on an upturned plate. Whisk the ingredients for the icing together in a bowl, colouring it, if you like. Coat the top of the cake using a spoon, allowing the icing to run down the sides. Transfer it to a small board or a plate, scatter the rose petals over the top and any extra around the outside. Leave the icing to set for 1–2 hours. This cake keeps well for a couple of days.

The two off-the-shelf cakes that never fail to tempt in our house are sticky ginger and layered walnut sponges sandwiched with buttercream. This is my take on the latter.

layered espresso walnut loaf

Cake

225g self-raising flour
225g light muscovado sugar
$1/2$ teaspoon sea salt
225ml groundnut oil
4 medium eggs, separated
50ml espresso or very strong filter coffee, cooled
50ml milk
75g nibbed or chopped walnuts

Filling

Espresso cream (see page 35)

Icing

100g icing sugar, sifted, plus a little extra
    for dusting
1 tablespoon espresso or very strong filter coffee
6–8 walnut halves to decorate, optional

Makes 1 x 22cm loaf

Preheat the oven to 170°C fan/190°C/gas mark 5 and butter a 22cm (1.3l) loaf tin. Sift the flour, sugar and salt into a large bowl. Add the oil, egg yolks, espresso and milk and beat until smooth with a wooden spoon. Whisk the egg whites until stiff (I use an electric whisk for this) and fold into the mixture in two goes. Stir in the nibbed walnuts and transfer the mixture to the cake tin, smoothing the surface. Give the tin several sharp taps on the worktop to allow any bubbles to rise. Bake for 50–55 minutes or until a skewer inserted into the centre comes out clean. Leave the cake to cool in the tin for a few minutes, then run a knife around the edge and turn it onto a wire rack. Place it the right way up and leave to cool. If not icing it immediately, wrap it in clingfilm.

Slit the cake into three layers, cutting the first just below the top line of the tin to take into account the risen surface. Spread the espresso cream over the lower two layers and sandwich together.

To make the icing, blend the icing sugar and coffee together and drizzle down the centre of the cake, smoothing it towards the sides using a palette knife. Don't worry about completely covering the surface, or if it trickles down the sides. Decorate the top with the walnut halves, then dust over a little icing sugar using a tea strainer. Leave to set for 1 hour.

The recipe for this cake hails from the West Country where it's a traditional teatime treat.

somerset apple cake

2 Granny Smith apples

A couple of squeezes of lemon juice

175g golden caster sugar

175g unsalted butter, diced

3 medium eggs, separated

175g ground almonds

1 teaspoon baking powder, sifted

2 tablespoons apple brandy or calvados (optional)

Icing sugar for dusting

Makes 1 x 20cm cake

Peel, quarter and core the apples. Slice two of the quarters wafer thin, toss with a squeeze of lemon juice in a bowl and set aside. Slice the remaining apple quarters more thickly. Transfer to a bowl, toss again with a squeeze of lemon, and sprinkle over 1 tablespoon sugar. Toss to coat the slices and put aside for 10 minutes while you prepare the cake mixture.

Preheat the oven to 140°C fan/160°C/gas mark 3 and butter a 20cm cake tin 9cm deep with a removeable base. Cream the butter and remaining sugar together until light and fluffy in a food processor. Beat in the egg yolks, then incorporate the ground almonds and baking powder, working the mixture as little as possible, then transfer the mixture to a large bowl.

Stiffly whisk the egg whites in another bowl and fold them in two goes into the cake mixture. Add the apple brandy or calvados, if using, and any juice given out by the thickly sliced apples. Drain these thoroughly on kitchen paper and gently fold them into the mixture. Transfer it to the prepared cake tin and smooth the surface. Drain the reserved finely sliced apple and arrange on top of the cake, sticking some of the slices in at an angle. Bake for 1 hour 15 minutes or until golden and a skewer inserted into the centre comes out clean.

Run a knife around the edge of the cake and leave it to cool for several hours. Dust with icing sugar. Being such a moist cake it keeps well in a covered container, and can be reheated if you want to serve it warm. It is delicious with a dollop of Calvados Cream (see page 81).

Crumble on top of cake is a perfect match of opposites, separated here by a juicy layer of cherries. This is a cake that is equally at home with tea or coffee, as it is with a glass of sticky (dessert) wine for pud and a dollop of crème fraîche.

cherry crumble cake

Cake

100g unsalted butter, diced
100g golden caster sugar
1 medium egg
90ml milk
125g self-raising flour, sifted
$1/2$ teaspoon baking powder, sifted
Finely grated zest of 1 lemon
250g black cherries, pitted

Crumble

90g plain flour
50g golden caster sugar
$1/2$ teaspoon ground cinnamon
90g unsalted butter, chilled and diced
25g organic porridge oats

Makes 1 x 20cm cake

Preheat the oven to 180°C fan/200°C/gas mark 6 and butter a 20cm cake tin 9cm deep with a removeable base. To make the cake, cream the butter and sugar in a food processor until light and fluffy. Add the egg, then incorporate the milk, flour, baking powder and lemon zest. Spoon the mixture into the prepared tin and smooth the surface.

To make the crumble, combine the flour, sugar, cinnamon and butter in a food processor and whizz until the mixture just starts to form large crumbs (or do this by hand). Transfer the mixture from the food processor to a bowl and stir in the oats.

Scatter the cherries over the surface of the cake, top with the crumble mixture and bake for 55–60 minutes or until a skewer inserted into the centre comes out clean. Run a knife around the edge of the cake. It can be served warm, about 30 minutes out of the oven, or at room temperature.

There are two takes on the strawberries here: if you want to be adult and organised, steep them in liqueur overnight. For an instant sauce, better suited to children, use 200g strawberry jam as below, stirring in 2 tablespoons lemon juice in lieu of the alcohol, before adding the strawberries. I like the cake best about 15 minutes out of the oven or just-cooled. It can also be reheated for 20 minutes in a moderate oven wrapped in foil.

polenta cake with macerated strawberries

Macerated strawberries
450g strawberries, hulled and quartered
4 tablespoons kirsch or dessert wine
125g strawberry jam

Cake
200g unsalted butter, diced
200g caster sugar
4 medium eggs
Finely grated zest and juice of 2 lemons
150g plain flour
1 teaspoon baking powder
150g fine-ground polenta
Icing sugar for dusting

Makes 1 x 20cm cake

Place the strawberries in a bowl, drizzle over the kirsch or wine, cover with clingfilm and chill for several hours or overnight, stirring at least once. Remove the strawberries from the fridge 30–60 minutes before serving. Gently warm the jam in a small pan until it begins to liquify, then pass through a sieve. Blend the macerating liquid into the jam, pour back over the fruit, stirring to coat.

Preheat the oven to 170°C fan/190°C/gas mark 5 and butter a 20cm cake tin 9cm deep with a removeable base. Cream the butter and sugar together in a food processor and incorporate the eggs, one by one, then the lemon zest and juice. Sift the flour and baking powder together and incorporate into the mixture, then the polenta. Transfer the mixture to the cake tin, smoothing the surface with a spoon. Bake for 35-40 minutes or until a skewer inserted into the centre comes out clean. Don't worry about the surface being golden. Run a knife around the edge of the cake and remove the collar. Dust the surface with icing sugar. Serve slices with the macerated strawberries and sauce spooned over.

pain d'épice

Divine toasted under the grill, with raspberry jam. Watch it carefully though – it burns easily.

125g plain flour, sifted

150g icing sugar, sifted

1 1/2 teaspoons ground cinnamon, sifted

2 teaspoons baking powder, sifted

175g unsalted butter, softened

4 medium eggs

Raspberry or strawberry jam, to serve (optional)

Makes 1 x 22cm loaf

Preheat the oven to 170°C fan/190°C/gas mark 5 and butter a 22cm (1.3l) loaf tin. Put all the ingredients except the jam in a food processor and cream together. Transfer to the tin, smooth the surface, and bake for 45 minutes or until a skewer inserted into the centre comes out clean. Run a knife round the edge and turn it the right way up onto a wire rack to cool.

dream cakes

These are 'oohh-aahhh' special occasion cakes, gloriously girly but not off-limits to blokes (think those ambitious – male – French patissiers who create great Alps of gâteaux to be admired in their shop windows). We're talking show-off time, cakes as fashionable art or even sculpture. You can pile them high, see the Towering Alaska, stack them deep, display them wide: all that is essential is good, basic flavours under the layers of catwalk-quality decoration meant to earn that round of applause (one cake here looks like a red-carpet dress Barbie ordered from a Paris show).

The trimmings used to be a secret shared only in the closed world of professional icing bags, syringes and nozzles, but now bling for home-made cakes has arrived in cookshops and even supermarkets. It changes with fashions, too – silver balls and tiny statuary have given way to sprinkles, glitter and grafitti done with writing icing tubes. What matters is aspiration – make a big statement – and a dramatic but simple design. Remember: it'll all be eaten by the end of the meal, it's not going up on a plinth in a fancy gallery. Not tempted? You're on the wrong page.

This gets its name from the medley of sponge, jam, cream and meringues that is reminiscent of baked alaska. It's deliciously extravagant – worthy of a stage set.

towering alaska

Meringues

3 medium egg whites

120g caster sugar

Pink and blue food colouring, paste or liquid

Cake

4 medium eggs, separated

175g caster sugar

225g ground almonds

1 teaspoon baking powder, sifted

Filling

200g black cherry jam, stirred until smooth

300ml whipping cream, whipped

Makes 1 x 23cm cake

To make the meringues, preheat the oven to 120°C fan/140°C/gas mark 1. Put the egg whites in a large bowl and whisk them until they rise into a froth the consistency of shaving foam. Sprinkle over 1 heaped tablespoon of the sugar at a time, whisking well with each addition until you have a smooth, glossy meringue. Divide the mixture into two, and colour each one a different pastel shade with a little food colouring.

Line one or two baking trays with baking paper. Drop teaspoons of the mixture onto the paper leaving plenty of space between each meringue. Put the meringues in the oven and turn it down to 100°C fan/120°C/gas mark 1/2. Cook for 1 hour – if you are using two trays, switch them around halfway through. The meringues are done when they are crisp on the outside and, if you tap the base, it should sound hollow within. Remove and leave them to cool.

To make the cake, turn the oven up to 180°C fan/200°C/gas mark 6 and butter a 23cm cake tin 9cm deep with a removeable base. Whisk the egg yolks and sugar together, without allowing the mixture to become too pale and thick. Stiffly whisk the egg whites and gently fold them into the mixture in three goes. Fold in the ground almonds and the baking powder.

Pour the cake mixture into the tin and give it a couple of taps on the worktop to bring up any air bubbles. Bake for 30–35 minutes or until the top feels springy to the touch, the sides are shrinking away from the tin and a skewer inserted into the centre comes out clean. Remove the collar from the cake and leave to cool.

Place the cake on a serving plate and spread the surface with the jam, right to the edge. Smooth the whipped cream on top, then the meringues. Serve as soon as possible, though the cake will keep well in a cool place for a couple of hours.

tangerine dream

Cake

350g skinned hazelnuts

4 medium eggs, separated

150g golden caster sugar

1 1/2 teaspoons baking powder, sifted

Filling

Finely grated zest of 1 orange,
    plus 1 tablespoon juice

1 tablespoon lemon juice

2 medium organic eggs

60g unsalted butter

90g golden caster sugar

300g mascarpone

Frosting

1 medium organic egg white

180–200g icing sugar, sifted

1 teaspoon lemon juice

Few drops of orange food colouring,
    paste or liquid (or a mixture of red
    and yellow)

Mini jellied orange and lemon slices
    or diamonds

Makes 1 x 20cm cake

To make the orange curd for the filling, place all the ingredients except the mascarpone in a bowl set over a pan of simmering water. Whisk until the butter melts, then continue to whisk for a further 1–2 minutes until the mixture thickens into a custard. Pass it through a sieve into a bowl, cover with clingfilm and chill for a couple of hours until it sets.

To make the cake, heat the oven to 160°C fan/180°C/gas mark 4 and butter two 20cm cake tins at least 5cm deep with a removeable base. Grind the hazelnuts as finely as possible in a food processor. Whisk the egg whites in a large bowl until stiff, and whisk the egg yolks and sugar in another large bowl until creamy and blended. Fold the egg whites into the yolk and sugar mixture in two goes, then fold in the ground hazelnuts, again in two goes, and finally the baking powder. Pour a third of the mixture into one tin and the remaining two-thirds into the other. Give each tin a sharp tap on the worktop to bring up any large bubbles and bake for 30 and 40 minutes respectively, until firm in the centre and shrinking from the sides. Run a knife around the edge of each cake and leave them to cool completely.

Blend 150g orange curd (enjoy the remainder on toast) and the mascarpone to make the filling. For the frosting, whisk the egg white until risen using an electric whisk, then gradually whisk in the icing sugar until it is really stiff. Add the lemon juice, colour it a very pale orange with a little food colouring, then whisk for a minute or two longer.

Remove both cakes from their bases with a bread knife and trim the top off the smaller cake. Slit the larger cake in two, and spread half the filling over the base with a palette knife. Put the small cake layer on top, then the rest of the filling and the final cake layer. Spread the frosting over the top, right to the edges, then bring it up into peaks using a table knife. Decorate with jellied orange and lemon slices and set aside in a cool place for a couple of hours for the icing to set. If not serving it immediately, cover and chill it, and remove it from the fridge about 30 minutes before serving. It will keep for several days.

white chocolate mousse cake with red fruits

Mousse and fruit

400ml double cream
250g white chocolate, broken
    into pieces
125g raspberries
125g strawberries, hulled
    and halved or quartered
Icing sugar for dusting

Sponge

100g plain flour
Pinch of sea salt
6 large eggs
150g caster sugar

Makes 1 x 23cm cake

Bring the cream to the boil in a non-stick saucepan. Pour half over the chocolate in a bowl, leave for 1–2 minutes to soften, stir until it is almost melted, then pour the rest over and stir until smooth. Leave to cool, then cover and chill for at least 1 hour.

To make the sponge, preheat the oven to 180°C fan/200°C/gas mark 6 and butter two 23cm sandwich or deep cake tins with removeable bases. Sift the flour into a bowl and add the salt. Put the eggs and sugar in a bowl and whisk for 8–10 minutes using an electric whisk, until the mixture is almost white and mousse-like. (You can do this in a food processor using the whisking attachment, in which case reduce the time to about 5 minutes.) Lightly fold in the flour in two goes. Divide the mixture between the prepared tins, and give them a couple of sharp taps on the worktop to eliminate any large bubbles. Bake for 12–14 minutes or until the sponge is light golden, springy to the touch, shrinking from the sides and a skewer inserted into the centre comes out clean. The cake on the lower shelf may need a few minutes longer. Remove from the oven and run a knife around the edges to loosen them, then leave to cool, when the cakes will sink a little.

Given the delicacy of the sponge, the cake is best assembled on the plate you want to serve it from. Loosen both sponges using a palette knife and put one on a plate. Using an electric whisk beat the mousse mixture until it forms soft but firm peaks, taking care to stop whisking before it turns grainy. As long as it is thick enough to spread it will firm up further on chilling. Spread a third of it over the surface of one sponge, sandwich with the second sponge and spread another third over the top. Use the remainder to coat the sides of the cake – you may need a small knife to do the bottom sponge. Clean the edges of the plate with kitchen paper, and chill the cake for a couple of hours for the mousse to set. If keeping it any longer than this, cover with clingfilm at this point.

Just before serving, scatter the raspberries and strawberries over the top of the cake, mainly towards the centre, and dust with icing sugar. Like a trifle, the cake itself should be served lightly chilled, but the fruit is nicest at room temperature.

banana passion

A glammed-up banana cake: three beautifully moist layers with cream cheese frosting in between. But you could just as easily make it as the usual two-layer affair if you prefer.

Cake

2 very ripe bananas, peeled and mashed

1 x 227g tin pineapple (or 130g fresh pineapple), drained and coarsely chopped

200ml groundnut oil

250g golden caster sugar

3 medium eggs, separated

3 tablespoons milk

100g chopped pecan nuts

200g plain flour

2 teaspoons baking powder

3/4 teaspoon each ground ginger and cinnamon

Frosting

180g unsalted butter, softened

150g icing sugar, sifted

450g low-fat cream cheese

1 teaspoon vanilla extract

Barbie sprinkles and glitter writing icing

Makes 1 x 20cm cake

Preheat the oven to 170°C fan/190°C/gas mark 5 and butter a 20cm cake tin 9cm deep with a removeable base. Combine the banana and pineapple in a large bowl, whisk in the oil and sugar, then whisk in the egg yolks and milk, and fold in the nuts. Sift the flour and baking powder together and stir this into the mixture, and then the spices. Stiffly whisk the egg whites in a bowl and fold them into the mixture in two goes. Pour the mixture into the tin, smoothing the surface, and bake for 60–70 minutes or until the sides are shrinking away from the tin and a skewer inserted into the centre comes out clean. Run a knife around the edge of the cake and leave it to cool.

To make the frosting, cream the butter and icing sugar in a food processor. Remove the butter icing to a bowl, and blend with the cream cheese and vanilla extract until smooth.

Leaving the cake on the tin base, slit into three layers with a bread knife. Sandwich together, spreading 2–3 tablespoons frosting over the two bottom layers with a palette knife. Coat the top and sides of the cake with the remaining frosting – you will need more on the top than the sides, which won't show once they're decorated. Use the tiny bead-like Barbie sprinkles to coat the sides, and festoon the top with glitter writing icing (in several colours) and scatter a few more sprinkles in the centre.

Cover the cake with clingfilm and chill for 1 hour for the frosting to set. If chilling it any longer than this, remove from the fridge 30 minutes before serving. It keeps well for several days.

lime and coconut délice

Cake

350g desiccated coconut, plus a little extra for decorating

6 medium eggs, separated

250g golden caster sugar

1$^{1}/_{2}$ teaspoons baking powder, sifted

Mousse

4 sheets (approx. 12g) leaf gelatine, or 1 x 11g sachet

Zest and juice of 2 limes (if using a zester, finely chop the zest)

450ml double cream

450g Greek yogurt

125g icing sugar, sifted, plus a little extra for decorating

Green food colouring, paste or liquid

4 physalis, petals pulled back, to decorate

Makes 1 x 20cm cake

Preheat the oven to 180°C fan/200°C/gas mark 6 and butter two 20cm cake tins 9cm deep with a removeable base. Grind the desiccated coconut to a coarse meal in a food processor. Whisk the egg whites in a large bowl until stiff using an electric whisk. Whisk the egg yolks and caster sugar in another large bowl until creamy. Fold the egg whites into the yolks in two goes, and then the ground coconut and the baking power. Pour two-thirds of the cake mixture into one tin, and a third into the other. Bake them for 25 and 20 minutes respectively or until risen and firm, and the sides are shrinking away from the tin. Run a knife around the edges and leave to cool.

To prepare the mousse, cut the gelatine sheets into wide strips and soak them in a small bowl of cold water for 5 minutes. Drain off the water, pour in the lime juice to submerge the strips, and stand the bowl in another bowl of just-boiled water. Stir for a few minutes to dissolve, then leave to cool to room temperature. If using a sachet, sprinkle the powder onto 4 tablespoons boiling water in a small bowl, leave for 3–4 minutes and then stir to dissolve. If it has not completely dissolved, stand the bowl in another bowl of just-boiled water for a few minutes, then stir again. Leave to cool to room temperature.

Combine the cream, yogurt, lime zest and icing sugar, and colour it a pale eau-de-nil with a little food colouring. Stir in the gelatine solution, combining it thoroughly.

To assemble the cake, trim the surface of the smaller cake using a bread knife and place it back in the tin. Trim away the surface of the larger one, too, then slit it into two layers. Spoon a third of the mousse over the cake in the tin, lay the top of the larger cake over it, then smooth over another third of the mousse. Put the final cake layer in place, base upwards, then smooth over the remainder of the mousse. Cover the cake with clingfilm and chill for at least 4 hours or overnight. To complete the decoration, sprinkle a little desiccated coconut around the rim of the cake. Run a knife around the collar of the tin and remove it. Place the physalis in the centre of the cake and dust them with icing sugar. Serve the cake chilled.

The sugary pink icing is balanced by a filling of fresh raspberries and mascarpone – that much sharper and more perfumed than the usual buttercream.

raspberry mascarpone layer cake

Cake

6 medium eggs, separated
250g caster sugar
350g ground almonds
1¹/₂ teaspoons baking powder, sifted

Filling

250g mascarpone
25g icing sugar, sifted, plus
  extra for dusting
1 teaspoon vanilla extract
250g raspberries, coarsely mashed, plus a
  handful of whole ones to decorate

Icing

150g icing sugar, sieved
2 tablespoons fresh orange juice, sieved
Pink food colouring, paste
  or liquid

Makes 1 x 23cm cake

To prepare the sponges, preheat the oven to 180°C fan/200°C/gas mark 6 and butter two 23cm sandwich or deep cake tins with a removeable base. Whisk the egg yolks and sugar together but don't let the mixture become too pale and thick. Stiffly whisk the egg whites and gently fold them into the mixture in three goes. Fold in the ground almonds and the baking powder.

Pour two-thirds of the cake mixture into one of the tins, and the remaining third into the other. Give them a couple of taps on the worktop to bring up any air bubbles. Bake the larger cake for 30–35 minutes and the smaller one for 20–25 minutes or until the top feels springy to the touch, the sides are shrinking away from the tin and a skewer inserted into the centre comes out clean. Remove the collars from the cakes and leave them to cool.

Blend the mascarpone, icing sugar and vanilla extract in a bowl then stir in the raspberries. In another bowl mix the ingredients for the icing until smooth.

Slit the larger cake in half and invert the top half of the cake as the base, placing it on a cake board or serving plate. Spread with half the filling. Trim the surface off the smaller cake, place as the middle layer of the cake and spread with the remaining filling. Put the bottom half of the large cake, cut-side up, as the final layer. Coat the top of the cake with the icing using a palette knife, and pile the raspberries in the centre. Dust them with icing sugar and set aside in a cool place for 2 hours for the icing to set.

This is a great one to send into class or on a picnic, and will stretch to a fairly large number depending on how small you cut the squares.

kiddies' dream traybake

Cake

75g cocoa powder

3/4 teaspoon bicarbonate of soda

4 medium eggs

370g light muscovado sugar

180ml vegetable oil

200g self-raising flour, sifted

Icing

150g dark chocolate (about 50% cocoa solids), broken into pieces

3 tablespoons milk

Smarties and 100s and 1000s to decorate

Makes approx. 20 squares

Whisk the cocoa with 200ml boiling water, whisk in the bicarbonate of soda and leave to cool for about 20 minutes. Preheat the oven to 160°C fan/180°C/gas mark 4, and butter or oil a 23 x 30 x 4cm traybake tin (there is no need to line it unless you are planning on turning the cake out whole).

Whisk together the eggs, sugar and oil, then stir in the flour, then the cocoa solution. Pour the mixture into the prepared tin and bake for 30-40 minutes or until risen and firm, and a skewer inserted into the centre comes out clean. Run a knife around the edge of the cake and leave to cool.

To make the icing, gently melt the chocolate with the milk in a bowl set over a pan with a little simmering water in it, stirring until smooth, and using the back of a spoon or palette knife coat the surface of the cake. Scatter over some Smarties and 100s and 1000s, and leave for a couple of hours to set. Cut into squares to serve.

This is the cheat of the pack, you can use any combination of ready-made sorbet and ice-cream here, whatever you feel complements each other. I've tried it with orange ice-cream and raspberry sorbet, and pistachio ice-cream with peach sorbet, both of which were delicious. For a child-friendly version, omit the rum and increase the orange juice to 270ml.

ice-cream cake

Remove the sorbet and ice-cream from the freezer about 30–45 minutes before assembling the cake – it needs to be putty-soft.

Combine the rum and orange juice in a shallow bowl. Dip a few sponge fingers into the liquid at a time, so that they just start to give without feeling sodden – they should retain a crisp biscuity heart. Use these to line the bottom of a 22cm (1.3l) loaf tin, in a row, placing them sugared-side down. Now line the sides with biscuits, dipping them as before and standing them upright.

Spoon the sorbet into the bottom of the tin, pressing down with a spoon to exclude any air gaps. Repeat with the ice-cream: the sorbet should account for three-quarters of the depth of the tin and the ice-cream for the remaining quarter.

Using a bread knife, carefully saw off the tops of the biscuits, holding the tips in place so they don't move around too much. Cover the surface with clingfilm and return to the freezer for 1 hour. This is just the right length of time for the ice-cream to firm up again, without the orange liquid freezing. If however you are refreezing it in a fridge-top ice-box, it may take 2, even 3, hours to firm up again.

Remove from the freezer, run a knife around the edge of the mould and turn the ice-cream out onto a plate. Serve it in slices (you may want to discard the very ends). If you like, decorate each plate with a couple of physalis with their petals pulled back.

1 x 500ml tub orange, raspberry or mango sorbet

$^2/_3$ x 500ml tub orange or other fruit ice-cream

90ml dark rum

180ml fresh orange juice, sieved

1 x 200g pack boudoir biscuits or sponge fingers

12 physalis (optional)

Makes 1 x 22cm cake

festive baking

These are cakes we can prepare as shared markers of holidays through the year – yet the day we make them is perhaps more important than the day on which they are traditionally eaten. For example, I delight in making the traditional rich fruitcake for Christmas, so that I can inhale that heady rum-soaked aroma of dried fruit, peel and nuts. But these days, when we've sugar enough in our diets all the time, the chances are that the cake will still be sitting in a tin in the spring, since nobody wants all that heaviness with icing on top. My answer, see the next page, is a much gooier, boiled fruit cake, with honey instead of sugar, updated with dried cherries (we have such a wide choice now of dried fruits, temperate and tropical, that sultanas and currants must take their turns).

You might also like to try the lighter, un-iced fruit cakes, or perhaps my mother's Chocolate Chestnut Log, which is mid-way between a cake and a pudding. Retain the idea of the holiday cake, but maybe modernise the recipes to suit today's lighter tastes. For Easter, consider Orange Marzipan Cake instead of straight Simnel; for Valentine's, anything baked with love says it just as beautifully as flowers.

This is my stock special occasion fruit cake, the sour cherries and cranberry juice bring it to life. There are no eggs, and the cake relies on honey to sweeten it. Choose a light mild honey, though, rather than one that's dark and resinous.

Like most fruitcakes, this can be matured to develop its flavour. Wrap it in a double layer of baking paper and then foil, and feed with teaspoons of calvados or brandy at weekly intervals (pierce the surface first with a skewer). But equally it can be eaten as soon as it is made – it'll be that little bit more crumbly, but that's no bad thing. If you need a shortcut, forgo the fondant icing and use ready to roll icing.

christmas cake

Heat the butter, honey and cranberry juice in a medium saucepan until the butter melts, stir in the cherries and raisins, bring to the boil and simmer over a low heat for 5 minutes. Stir in the bicarbonate of soda – the mixture will sizzle furiously – then leave to cool for 10 minutes.

Heat the oven to 140°C fan/160°C/gas mark 3, and butter a 20cm cake tin 9cm deep with a removeable base. Line the bottom with baking paper, and butter this too. Combine the flour, ground almonds and nutmeg in a large mixing bowl, tip in the fruit mixture and beat to combine them. Fold in the peel and transfer the mixture to the cake tin, smoothing the surface. Tear off a sheet of baking paper large enough to cover the surface of the cake and extend about half way down the sides of the tin. Cut a small circle in the centre, about 2cm in diameter, butter the surface that will come in contact with the cake as it rises, lay it over the top of the tin and tie it in place with string. Bake the cake for 2½ hours, or until a skewer inserted into the centre comes out clean. Run a knife around the edge to remove the collar and leave the cake to cool on the base.

Remove the cake from the base and peel off the paper on the bottom. Set the cake on a plate or board. Gently heat the jam in a small saucepan, pass it

Cake

300g unsalted butter

300g runny honey (e.g. acacia)

300ml cranberry juice

350g dried sour cherries

325g raisins

1 teaspoon bicarbonate of soda

150g plain flour, sifted

150g ground almonds

½ teaspoon freshly grated nutmeg

100g finely diced candied orange peel*

Marzipan and icing

75g apricot jam

500g natural marzipan

500g icing sugar, sifted

1 medium organic egg white

1 heaped tablespoon of liquid glucose

Brandy for brushing

Food colouring, paste or liquid (optional)

Silver balls to decorate

Makes 1 x 20cm cake

through a sieve and lightly glaze the cake using a
pastry brush. Measure the cake from the base of
one side to the base of the other. Thinly roll out
the marzipan on a worktop dusted with icing sugar
into a circle a little bigger than this – it should be
about 30cm in diameter. Loosen the marzipan
with a palette knife every now and again, and
sprinkle the surface with more icing sugar if
necessary. Roll the marzipan around the rolling
pin, lift it up and carefully lay it over the cake,
letting it drape down the sides. Press it to the
sides of the cake, cutting out darts where folds
appear and smoothing these with your fingers,
then trim it at base level. Set the cake aside
overnight for the marizpan to semi-dry.

To make the fondant icing, put the icing sugar,
egg white and liquid glucose in the bowl of a food
processor and whizz until the mixture looks
crumb-like. Tip it onto a board and bring it
together into a ball. It will look quite dry at this
point, but knead it with your hands for 5–10
minutes until very smooth and pliable. Roll it out
as you did the marzipan. Brush the surface of the
marzipan with brandy before laying the icing in place and trimming it in the
same way.

Using the trimmings, cut out some star shapes for the centre of the cake,
brushing the base of these with brandy to secure them to the top. You could
colour some of the icing with a little food colouring to make little balls as you
wish, or decorate with silver. Set the cake aside to dry out for at least a couple
of hours. Like most fruitcakes this will keep well in a tin or covered container.

* Look out for candied peel sold by the segment, it's often that much tastier
than ready-diced.

A Bûche de Noël is the French equivalent of our Christmas pudding, and comes in many different forms. This particular mousse-like log was a childhood favourite and still is. The French would really go to town with the coloured icing, Santa and reindeers. But there's enough kitsch going on at Christmas, so more simply you can throw some chocolate leaves over and dust them with icing sugar. Adults may appreciate a spoonful of boozy cream (see page 81).

chocolate chestnut log

100g dark chocolate (70% cocoa solids),
  broken into pieces
50g unsalted butter, diced
1 x 435g tin unsweetened chestnut purée
75g golden caster sugar
100g extra-thick double cream
1 teaspoon vanilla extract

Dark chocolate leaves, to decorate
Icing sugar for dusting

Makes 1 x 20cm log

Put the chocolate and butter in a bowl set over a pan of simmering water and gently melt them, stirring now and again until smooth and amalgamated. Remove the bowl from the heat and leave to cool to room temperature.

Put the chestnut purée, sugar, cream and vanilla extract in a food processor and whizz until creamy, add the cooled chocolate mixture and whizz again until you have a silky purée. It should be the consistency of whipped butter icing, firm enough to form into a log. If it seems a little loose (the consistency of chestnut purée can vary), simply transfer the mixture to a bowl, cover and chill until it firms up sufficiently to shape.

Next you need a stand for the log, a minimum of 20 x 8cm. You could use a small chopping board, otherwise the piece of card that comes inside the chocolate bar wrapper. Wrap this in foil and pile the chocolate chestnut mixture along its length. Run the tines of a fork along the length of the log to simulate a bark pattern, and smooth the ends with a palette knife. Decorate the forked surface with chocolate leaves, and place in the fridge for several hours, or overnight, until set. I like the log best about 30 minutes out of the fridge. Dust it with icing sugar, if wished, just before serving.

Christmas has as much to do with scents and flavours as lights on a tree – here, oranges, dried fruit, nuts and rum mingle together. I agonised over how to include marzipan in a way that would appeal to those who normally surreptitiously remove it; this has just the thinnest layer, inside the cake rather than out, which renders it deliciously gooey rather than dry. Try to buy a block of marzipan – ready-rolled is too thick, though you can always take out a rolling pin. Hand any trimmings to the kids with a set of pastry cutters.

orange marzipan cake

Shortbread

90g unsalted butter, diced
40g golden caster sugar
75g plain flour
50g ground almonds

Cake

225g unsalted butter, diced
225g golden caster sugar
4 medium eggs, plus 1 egg yolk
90ml dark rum
75g sultanas
75g raisins
225g self-raising flour
1 teaspoon baking powder
200g marzipan
Icing sugar for dusting
75g coarse-cut marmalade
20g flaked almonds
20g pine nuts

Makes 1 x 20cm cake

Put all the ingredients for the shortbread in a food processor and reduce to crumbs, then keep the motor running until the mixture comes together into a ball. It will be very soft and sticky at this point, but press it into the base of a 20cm cake tin 9cm deep with a removeable base, laying a sheet of clingfilm over the top and smoothing it with your fingers. Cover the surface of the tin with clingfilm and chill for 1 hour.

Preheat the oven to 170°C fan/190°C/gas mark 5. To make the cake, put the butter and caster sugar in the food processor and cream for several minutes until very pale and fluffy. Add the eggs and the yolk one at a time, scraping down the bowl if necessary. Incorporate the rum. Pour this mixture into a large bowl. Toss the sultanas and raisins with a little flour to coat them. Sift the remaining flour and baking powder over the cake mixture and fold in, then the dried fruit.

Thinly roll out the marzipan on a worktop dusted with icing sugar until it is transparently thin, about 2mm thick. Cut out a 20cm circle (the size of your cake tin), and spread the marmalade over the surface with a palette knife, evenly distributing the peel. Lay this over the shortbread base marmalade-side up, then spread the cake mixture on top. Scatter over the nuts and bake for 60–70 minutes or until a skewer inserted into the centre comes out clean.

Run a knife around the edge of the cake and leave to cool. Dust with icing sugar before serving. The cake keeps well in a covered container for several days.

A lovely light fruitcake, courtesy of a San Franciscan, Carol Field, who specialises in artisanal Italian breads and pastries. Just a few currants set within a sponge scented with rum, and if you like you can steep them in the liquor overnight.

italian currant cake

225g unsalted butter, diced
225g golden caster sugar
4 medium eggs, plus 1 egg yolk
90ml rum, madeira or vin santo
1 teaspoon vanilla extract
200g currants
225g plain flour, sifted
1 teaspoon baking powder, sifted
35g flaked almonds
Icing sugar for dusting

Makes 1 x 22cm loaf

Preheat the oven to 170°C fan/190°C/gas mark 5 and butter and flour a 22cm (1.3l) loaf tin. Put the butter and sugar in a food processor and cream for several minutes until very pale and fluffy. Add the eggs and the yolk one at a time, scraping down the bowl if necessary. Incorporate the rum or wine and the vanilla and continue to process for a couple of minutes. Pour this mixture into a large bowl. Toss the currants with a little flour to coat them. Sift the remaining flour and baking powder over the cake mixture and gently fold in, then the currants. Transfer the mixture to the prepared tin, mounding it a little in the centre. Sprinkle the almonds over the top. (This may seem quite a lot of almonds but once the cake has risen they will spread out.) Bake the cake for 60–65 minutes or until it is golden and risen and a skewer inserted into the centre comes out clean. Leave it to cool in the tin for several minutes, then run a knife around the edge and turn it out onto a wire rack. Place it the right way up and leave to cool. Dust with icing sugar before serving.

naughty treats

In my over-indulged childhood you didn't have either rum butter or brandy cream, you had both. A bowl of these in the fridge over Christmas will see you through any number of teas and puds.

rum butter

175g unsalted butter, softened
175g icing sugar, sifted
6 tablespoons dark rum

Serves 6–8

Beat the butter and icing sugar together until light and fluffy. Gradually beat in the rum, until you have a smooth creamy butter. Transfer to a bowl, cover and chill until required. Remove the butter from the fridge about 20 minutes before serving.

calvados cream

A thick, sweet pouring cream laced with calvados: divine with warm Mince Pies or Somerset Apple Cake (see page 48). Don't buy a bottle of calvados especially though – use whatever the drinks cupboard offers.

225g crème fraîche
1–2 tablespoons calvados, armagnac, brandy or fruit eau-de-vie
50g icing sugar, sifted

Serves 6–8

Whisk the ingredients together in a bowl, cover and chill until required.

mincemeat

For me mincemeat is one of the quintessential tastes of Christmas. That first crumbly morsel of mince pie brings with it a host of sugared memories, when all Christmases were white and Santa could be relied upon to bring you what you asked for. Even though we all take full advantage of shop-bought mince pies in the run-up to the big day, for a little effort you can recreate the nostalgic scent of a batch of pies baking in the oven, safe in the knowledge they will beat anything you can buy hands down.

Mincemeat is one of those eccentric British confections, a blend of dried fruit and nuts, spices, brown sugar and brandy that is a masterpiece in its own right. Jars of mincemeat are not to be sniffed at, though I like to jazz them up with the help of a little extra spirit and lemon zest. Spoon a 400g jar of mincemeat into a bowl and stir in 1 tablespoon brandy or cognac, the finely grated zest of a lemon and a knifetip of ground cinnamon.

home-made mincemeat

150g currants

125g raisins

25g blanched almonds,
   finely chopped

1 knob of stem ginger,
   finely chopped

1 eating apple, peeled and grated

50g shredded suet (beef
   or vegetable)

1/4 teaspoon ground cinnamon

1/4 teaspoon ground nutmeg

Knife tip of ground cloves

Finely grated zest and juice
   of 1 lemon

2 tablespoons brandy

1 tablespoon dark muscovado
   sugar

Makes 500g

The joy of mincemeat is creating it to suit your own taste, so use this as a guideline. You may be partial to glacé cherries and candied peel, or prefer rum in lieu of brandy, orange instead of lemon.

Combine all the ingredients for the mincemeat in a bowl, cover and set aside for at least 12 hours.

open mince pies

To make the pastry place the flour and butter in a food processor, give it a quick burst at high speed to reduce it to a crumb-like consistency, then add the lemon zest and icing sugar and give it another quick burst. Add the egg yolks and enough milk to bring the dough together. Wrap it in clingfilm and chill for 1 hour or overnight.

Preheat the oven to 170°C fan/190°C/gas mark 5. It's easier to work with half the pastry at a time. Roll it out on a lightly floured worktop and, using a fluted pastry cutter, cut out circles to fit fairy-cake racks (ideally non-stick). Place in the tins and fill with 1 heaped teaspoon mincemeat. Roll the trimmings and cut out shapes (stars or Christmas trees) slightly smaller than the pie diameter and lay one in the centre of each pie. Bake for 15 minutes until the pastry is pale gold. Leave to cool, then dust with icing sugar and slip out of the tins. They can be served warm, about 20 minutes out of the oven, or reheated for 5 minutes at 150°C fan/170°C/gas mark 3. A dollop of Rum Butter or Calvados Cream (see page 81) is always a treat if you're serving them for pudding.

Pastry

450g plain flour
250g unsalted butter, chilled and diced
Finely grated zest of 1 lemon
150g icing sugar, sifted
2 small egg yolks
Milk

1 quantity of mincemeat (see facing page)
Icing sugar for dusting

Makes 2–3 dozen

My mother used to make something along these lines with the unlikely title of Sahara mincemeat, which became a great family favourite.

cranberry-mince shortcake

Shortcake

175g unsalted butter, diced
75g golden caster sugar
150g plain flour
1 teaspoon baking powder, sifted
100g ground almonds
4 medium eggs, separated

Topping

400g mincemeat
150g cranberries
Icing sugar for dusting

Makes 12

Preheat the oven to 160°C fan/180°C/gas mark 4 and butter a 30 x 23 x 4cm baking tin. Put the butter, sugar, flour, baking powder and ground almonds in a food processor and reduce to a crumb-like consistency. As they start to cling together add the egg yolks and continue to process to a sticky dough. Press the dough into the base of the cake tin by laying a sheet of clingfilm over the top and smoothing it with your fingers. Remove the clingfilm and bake the shortcake for 25–30 minutes until lightly golden and slightly risen.

Whisk the egg whites until stiff. Spoon the mincemeat into a bowl and fold in the whisked whites in two goes. Fold in 100g of the cranberries and smooth the mixture over the shortcake base. Scatter the remaining cranberries over the top and bake for 20–25 minutes until lightly coloured on the surface.

Remove and run a knife around the edge of the shortcake, then leave it to cool completely. Cut it into 12 squares, approx. 7cm, dust with icing sugar and transfer to a plate. The shortcake will also keep well in a covered container for several days. In this case dust it with icing sugar just before serving.

This creamy treacle tart is halfway to a pecan pie, a great recipe even outside the festive season, in which case you may like to leave off the stars. Some crème fraîche or a scoop of vanilla ice-cream would go down nicely.

treacle star tart

Pastry

230g plain flour

70g golden caster sugar

130g unsalted butter, chilled and diced

1 medium egg, separated

Milk

Filling

3 medium eggs, plus 2 egg yolks

Juice and finely grated zest of 1 lemon

300ml golden syrup

300ml double cream

100g pecan nuts

1 eating apple, peeled and grated

Icing sugar for dusting

Makes 1 x 23cm tart

Put the flour, sugar and butter in a food processor and give it a quick burst at high speed to reduce to a crumb-like consistency. Add the egg yolk and then, with the motor running, trickle in just enough milk for the dough to cling together in lumps. Transfer the pastry to a large bowl and bring it together into a ball with your hands. Wrap the pastry in clingfilm and chill for at least 1 hour, or overnight.

Preheat the oven to 180°C fan/200°C/gas mark 6. Lightly flour a worktop and roll out the pastry thinly. Line the base and sides of a 23cm loose-bottomed tart tin 4–6cm deep by slipping the base of the tin under the pastry and then into the tin, pressing it into the sides. Run a rolling pin across the top and reserve the trimmings. Line the case with foil, fill with baking beans or a dried pulse, and cook for 15 minutes. Remove the foil and beans, paint the case with egg white, patching any cracks with the trimmings, and cook for a further 5–10 minutes until evenly gold. If any cracks have reappeared patch them, then roll out the remaining trimmings slightly thicker than usual, and cut out 6 star shapes 6cm in diameter.

Turn the oven down to 150°C fan/170°C/gas mark 3. Whisk together the eggs, yolks, lemon juice and zest, add the golden syrup and cream and whisk until the mixture emulsifies. Finely chop the pecan nuts in the food processor, add to the mixture with the grated apple and mix well. Pour the mixture into the tart case, and decorate with the pastry stars. Place it on a baking tray and bake for 60 minutes. The filling should be lightly golden, puffy at the edges, and if you move the tart around it should wobble without showing any signs of being liquid. Remove and leave the tart to cool for a couple of hours. I also like it chilled (cover with clingfilm and place in the fridge for several hours or overnight). Just before serving, dust with icing sugar.

This is every bit as pretty as that cake in the local patisserie that's been on your mind as the easy answer to saying 'I love you' with zero effort. Boys get off pretty lightly with the old roses. But there's nothing like finding your loved one with floury patches smudged on her cheeks to convince him that it's the real thing.

raspberry valentine's cake

Cake

4 medium eggs, separated

175g golden caster sugar

250g ground almonds

1 teaspoon baking powder, sifted

Finely grated zest of 1 orange

Frosting

120g unsalted butter, softened

100g icing sugar, sifted

300g cream cheese

1 teaspoon vanilla extract

250g (approx.) raspberries

Handful of small unsprayed red rose petals (optional)

Icing sugar for dusting

Makes 1 x 23cm cake

Preheat the oven to 180°C fan/200°C/gas mark 6 and butter a 23cm cake tin 9cm deep with a removeable base. Whisk the egg whites in a large bowl until they are stiff. In another large bowl whisk the egg yolks and sugar until they are pale but not too white. Fold the whisked whites into the egg and sugar mixture in two goes, then fold in the ground almonds, again in two goes, and the baking powder and orange zest. Spoon the mixture into the prepared tin and smooth the surface with a spoon. Bake for 40 minutes or until golden and shrinking from the sides and a skewer inserted into the centre comes out clean. Run a knife around the edge of the cake and leave it to cool.

To make the frosting, place the butter and icing sugar in a food processor and blend until smooth and creamy. Transfer the buttercream to a large bowl and work in the cream cheese and vanilla extract.

Invert the cake onto a plate or board, keeping the base upwards. Make a heart template (see page 90), using the cake base to trace a circle, then cut out a heart from the cake using a large sharp knife.

Smooth the cream cheese frosting over the top and sides of the cake using a small palette knife. Arrange the raspberries on top of the cake, holes downwards, starting at the outer edge and working inwards. Transfer the cake to a serving plate or cake board. Scatter some rose petals over and around the cake if wished and dust with icing sugar. Unless you are serving it straight away, place the cake in a cool place for up to a couple of hours. Any longer than this, loosely cover it with clingfilm and chill it, in which case remove it from the fridge 30–60 minutes before serving.

Don't save this one for the new boy or girlfriend, it's great any time of the year, a moist marmalade sponge with orange butter icing. And if you want to go to town, a trip to one of the shops that specialises in edible decorations – or online – will provide the necessary bling (see page 9). Otherwise, physalis are the perfect colour.

heart of gold

Cake

180g unsalted butter, diced

180g golden caster sugar

3 medium eggs

5 tablespoons orange juice

250g self-raising flour, sifted

100g fine-shred marmalade

Sugared hearts and silver balls to decorate

Butter Icing

200g icing sugar, sifted

100g unsalted butter, softened

1 medium organic egg yolk

1 tablespoon orange juice, plus finely grated zest of 1 orange

1 tablespoon lemon juice

Yellow food colouring, paste or liquid

Makes 1 x 23cm cake

Preheat the oven to 160°C fan/180/gas mark 4 and butter a 23cm cake tin 9cm deep with a removeable base. Cream the butter and sugar together in a food processor until pale, then incorporate the eggs and then the juice; don't worry if the mixture appears curdled at this point. Transfer to a bowl and add the flour, then stir in the marmalade. Spoon the mixture into the prepared tin, smooth the surface and bake for 50 minutes or until a skewer inserted into the centre comes out clean. Run a knife around the edge of the cake and leave it to cool.

Make a heart template as described below and use this to cut the cake in a heart shape.

To prepare the butter icing, blend all the ingredients until creamy – you can do this in the food processor. Smooth it over the top and sides of the cake using a palette knife. Decorate with the hearts and silver balls. Place it on a serving plate or cake board and set aside in a cool place for a few hours for the butter icing to set. The cake will keep well for several days in a covered container.

heart template

To make a paper or card heart-shaped template, first cut out a circle the size of the cake (23cm). Now fold it in half and trace half a heart on the half moon. Cut it out with scissors and open it out. This will give you a perfectly symmetrical heart.

A halfway house between a fruit cake and a Victoria sponge, lightly set with a mixture of dried fruit and candied peel in the best of British traditions, with a saffron frosting on top.

easter fruit cake

Cake

225g unsalted butter, diced
225g golden caster sugar
4 medium eggs, plus 1 egg yolk
90ml medium sherry
200g luxury mixed fruit
225g plain flour
1 teaspoon baking powder
Finely grated zest of 1 lemon

Saffron frosting

120g unsalted butter, softened
100g icing sugar, sifted
300g low-fat cream cheese
Pinch of saffron filaments (about 30), ground in a pestle and mortar and infused in 1 tablespoon boiling water for 30 minutes
Chocolate mini eggs to decorate

Makes 20

Preheat the oven to 170°C fan/190°C/gas mark 5 and butter and flour a 30 x 23 x 4cm baking tin. Place the butter and sugar in a food processor and cream until very pale and fluffy. Add the eggs and the yolk one at a time, scraping down the bowl if necessary. Incorporate the sherry and continue to process for a couple more minutes. Pour this mixture into a large bowl. Toss the mixed fruit with a little flour to coat it. Sift the remaining flour and baking powder over the cake mixture and gently fold in, then the fruit and lemon zest. Transfer it to the prepared tin, smoothing the surface and bake for 30 minutes or until it is golden and shrinking from the sides. Leave it to cool in the tin for several minutes, then run a knife around the edge, turn it out onto a wire rack and allow to cool.

To make the frosting, place the butter and icing sugar in the food processor and blend until really creamy. Transfer it to a large bowl, thoroughly beat in the cream cheese, then the saffron infusion until the frosting is evenly yellow.

Place the cake the right way up on a tray. Smooth the saffron frosting over the top using a palette knife, and set aside in a cool place for 1 hour for the frosting to set. The cake can be made a day in advance, loosely covered with clingfilm and stored in a cool place. Shortly before serving, decorate it with mini eggs in whatever fashion takes your fancy; it could be a nest in the middle and a few scattered around. You can also tie a ribbon around the outside. Serve it cut into in squares.

easter egg brownies

This is a great way of surreptitiously using up any unwanted Easter eggs that linger after the event. Dark chocolate can be used in the cake mix itself, and dark or milk to decorate them.

Preheat the oven to 170°C fan/190°C/gas mark 5. You need a tin 30 x 19 x 4cm, or the equivalent in size. Provided it is non-stick there's no need to butter and flour it. To make the brownies, melt the chocolate with the butter in a bowl set over a pan of simmering water. Remove from the heat, add the sugar and stir to combine, then leave to cool slightly. Add the eggs and yolk to the chocolate mixture one by one, beating after each addition. The mixture should be very glossy. Gently fold in the ground almonds and salt, then sift over the flour and baking powder and fold in without overmixing. Stir in the coffee and fold in the brazil nuts.

Pour the chocolate mixture into the tin, and bake for 20–30 minutes until set but slightly wet in the centre. A skewer inserted in the centre should come out clean but with a few moist crumbs clinging. Run a knife around the edge of the tin, then leave the cake to cool.

To make the icing, melt the chocolate and butter as above, then leave to cool to room temperature. Cut the cake into 5cm squares. Smooth 1/2 teaspoon of the icing in the centre of each brownie and stick a couple of shards of Easter egg into each one. Leave for about 1 hour to set. Dust with icing sugar, then carefully remove the brownies to a plate using a palette knife.

Brownies

300g dark chocolate (minimum 70% cocoa solids), broken up

180g unsalted butter, diced

180g golden caster sugar

4 medium eggs, and 1 yolk

115g ground almonds

1/2 teaspoon sea salt

115g plain flour

1 heaped teaspoon baking powder

3 tablespoons espresso or strong black coffee

100g brazil nuts, thinly sliced

Icing

50g dark chocolate, broken up

15g unsalted butter

75g dark or milk chocolate Easter egg, broken into 2cm pieces

Icing sugar for dusting

Makes 15

So often it's the ideas or notions that seduce rather than the food itself, and I have always loved the idea of Battenburg. It's just that it has to be home-made. So here's all the colour of the fair, some peppery ginger jam between the layers and a saffron frosting, the only fat, so while luxurious it's not overly rich.

easter battenburg

Cake

6 medium eggs, separated

250g caster sugar

350g ground almonds

1¹/₂ teaspoons baking powder, sifted

Pink food colouring liquid

Frosting

75g flaked almonds

300g mascarpone

25g icing sugar, sifted, plus extra
2 teaspoons

Pinch of saffron filaments (about 30)
ground in a pestle and mortar
and infused in 1 tablespoon
boiling water for 30 minutes

300g ginger preserve

75g white chocolate mini eggs

Makes 1 x 23cm cake

Preheat the oven to 180°C fan/200°C/gas mark 6 and butter two 23cm sandwich or deep cake tins with a removeable base. Whisk the egg whites in a large bowl until stiff then whisk the egg yolks and sugar in another large bowl to blend them, they shouldn't be too pale and thick. Fold the whites into the egg mixture, then fold in the ground almonds in two goes and the baking powder.

Put a third of the mixture in one of the tins. Colour the remainder pink with food colouring, and transfer to the other tin. Bake the small cake for 20–25 minutes, the large one for 30–35 minutes or until the cake is shrinking from the sides and a skewer inserted into the centre comes out clean. Run a knife around the edge of each tin and leave to cool. Scatter the almonds over the base of a baking tray and toast them for 7–9 minutes until lightly golden, then leave them to cool.

To make the frosting, blend the mascarpone with the 25g icing sugar, then work in the saffron infusion. Put the extra 2 teaspoons icing sugar in a coffee grinder with 1–2 drops of pink food colouring and give it a whizz. The cake can be prepared to this point in advance, but finished within a few hours of eating.

To assemble the cake, trim off the top of the smaller cake with a bread knife, and slice the large one in two. Work the ginger preserve to a spreadable consistency, spread half of it over the base of the pink cake, top with the uncoloured cake, spread with the remaining preserve then sandwich with the top pink layer.

Use a palette knife to spread the mascarpone over the top then the sides of the cake. Press the almonds around the sides and place chocolate eggs in the centre. Dust the eggs with the pink icing sugar using a tea strainer.

Supermarkets do a good job of hero cakes so there's little
point in exhausting yourself if that's the order of the day.
The advantage of home-made birthday cake is it tastes
good too. I recall being enchanted by my first angel cake,
aged five. Fluffy and snowy white, it makes the perfect
backdrop for a shower of Smarties. And this one is
sufficiently light to merit a cream cheese frosting.

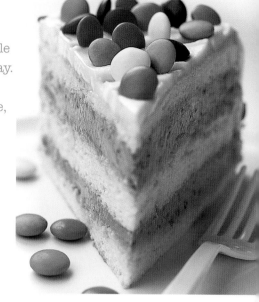

birthday angel smartie cake

Sponge

8 medium egg whites

$1/4$ teaspoon sea salt

1 teaspoon cream of tartar

250g icing sugar, sifted

140g plain flour, sifted

Filling

250g mascarpone

100g raspberry jam

Frosting

120g unsalted butter, softened

100g icing sugar, sifted

300g full-fat cream cheese

1 teaspoon vanilla extract

Several tubes of Smarties for decoration

Makes 1 x 23cm cake

Preheat the oven to 150°C fan/170°C/gas mark 3. Whisk the egg whites in a large
bowl with the salt and cream of tartar until they are risen. Sprinkle over the sugar,
2 tablespoons at a time, whisking well with each addition. Fold in the sifted flour
in three goes. Divide the mixture between two unbuttered 23cm cake tins 9cm
deep with a removeable base. Bake for 35–40 minutes or until lightly golden,
springy and shrinking from the sides. Run a knife around the edge of the cakes
and leave them to cool.

Blend the mascarpone with the jam. Put the butter and icing sugar for the
frosting in a food processor and blend until smooth and creamy. Transfer the
buttercream to a large bowl and work in the cream cheese and vanilla extract.

Slit one of the sponges in half with a bread knife. Slice the top off the other, and
cut the cake off its base to use as the middle layer. Spread half the raspberry
cream over one sponge, top with the middle layer, spread with the remaining
raspberry cream, then top with the third sponge. Smooth the frosting over the
top and sides of the cake with a palette knife. Transfer the cake to a 25cm cake
board. Chill the cake and remove it from the fridge 30–60 minutes before
serving. Decorate with Smarties near to the time of eating.

red velvet bonfire cake

Cake

120g unsalted butter

300g golden caster sugar

2 large eggs

300g plain flour, sifted

230g buttermilk

1 teaspoon sea salt

1 teaspoon vanilla extract

20g cocoa powder, sifted

1/2 teaspoon (approx.) red food
    colour paste

1 tablespoon white wine vinegar

1 teaspoon bicarbonate of soda

Frosting

180g unsalted butter, softened

150g icing sugar, sifted

450g full-fat cream or curd cheese

1 teaspoon vanilla extract

2 x 150g boxes mint or
    orange Matchmakers

Cocoa for dusting

Sparklers

Makes 1 x 20cm cake

Preheat the oven to 170°C fan/190°C/gas mark 5. Butter two (three if you have them) 20cm sandwich or deep cake tins with a removeable base, and line the base with baking paper. Cream the butter and sugar in a food processor until really light and fluffy. Add the eggs, one at a time, scraping down the sides of the bowl between each addition. Now add the flour in three goes, alternating with the buttermilk, beginning and ending with flour. Add the salt, vanilla extract and cocoa. Add the food colouring a knife tip at a time until the mixture is a dramatic dusky red: it needs about 1/2 teaspoon in all.

Mix the vinegar and bicarbonate of soda together (it will fizz), and add to the batter. Divide the mixture between the three tins or, if using two, add a third of the mixture to each one, bake these, and then bake the third sponge once the other two are cooling. (I weigh the mixture then divide it to get evenly thick sponges.) Bake the cakes for 20–25 minutes until shrinking from the sides and firm when pressed in the centre. Leave to cool for 10 minutes then turn the cakes out onto a wire rack, remove the paper and cool the right way up.

To make the frosting, cream the butter and icing sugar in a food processor then blend with the cream cheese and vanilla extract. Transfer to a bowl.

Stack the three sponges on top of each other. With a bread knife carve the stack into a cone, starting about an inch from the centre, to make the shape of a tall bonfire. (Trimmings can be saved for a trifle.) Separate out the layers again, spread 2–3 tablespoons frosting over the base layer using a palette knife, top with the middle layer and smooth over 1 1/2 tablespoons, then lay the top in place. Coat the sides of the cone with the remaining frosting, then stack the chocolate matchsticks upwards around the outside, breaking them in half towards the end to fill in the gaps. Dust the whole cake with cocoa and place on a plate or board. Cover with clingfilm and chill for 1 hour. If chilling it any longer than this, remove from the fridge 30 minutes before serving. It keeps well for several days. As a finale stick the top with sparklers and light them, and take it outside or into a darkened room.

chocolate cakes

Abandon guilt all ye who enter here, for this is the zone of the chocolate cake, which is both the essence of cakedom and its highest aspiration. The whole idea of a cake – a treat that is prepared in order to be shared, to celebrate the occasion – seems to demand the everyday grandeur of chocolate. The chocolate can be there as decoration (see my tips on page 9), since nothing swirls like it, drips like it or flows into that perfect smooth dark covering (wouldn't you love a handbag that exactly reproduced its sleek-matte quality?). Or it can contribute its richness to the texture – the simplest brownie is a fine demonstration of the power of chocolate. And always it offers its unique sensuous, dark and mysterious taste.

It's a creative substance, as well as being an addictive one. For all its extravagance it adjusts to styles high and low – imperial Sachertorte, Black Forest Victoria (once again reigning as queen-empress of the suburbs), even Swiss Roll with chocolate fudge for small boys of all ages. When in doubt, present chocolate. By the way, if you didn't manage to abandon the guilt, I include an almost fat-free chocolate gâteau.

This classic French take on a chocolate cake is a personal favourite: very dense but meltingly tender. It's deliciously messy and rustic, with high craggy sides and a fine crispy top. I like to smother it with a brandy-laced glaze and pile some Maltesers in the centre.

french and flourless

Cake

250g unsalted butter, diced

250g dark chocolate (approx. 50% cocoa solids), broken into pieces

5 medium eggs, separated

250g golden caster sugar

Glaze

150g dark chocolate, broken into pieces

2 tablespoons brandy

Maltesers to decorate

Icing sugar for dusting

Makes 1 x 20cm cake

Preheat the oven to 160°C fan/180°C/gas mark 4 and butter a 20cm cake tin 9cm deep with a removeable base. Melt the butter and chocolate in a bowl set over a pan with a little simmering water in it, stirring occasionally. At the same time, whisk the egg yolks with half the sugar for several minutes until pale and doubled in volume. You can do this in a food processor, then transfer the mixture to a large bowl.

Whisk the egg whites until stiff, then gradually whisk in the remaining sugar, a tablespoon at a time, whisking for about 20 seconds with each addition. By the end you should have a stiff glossy meringue.

Fold the chocolate and butter into the egg mixture, then the egg whites, in two goes. Pour the mixture into the prepared tin and bake for 50–60 minutes or until a skewer inserted into the centre comes out with just a few moist crumbs clinging. Run a knife around the edge and leave it to cool in the tin, when it will sink. Don't worry about the uneven appearance of the sides, some which will be higher than others. Its craggy appearance is all part of its charm. But if parts of the sides are very high, then simply break a little off to level them.

Melt the chocolate for the glaze with the brandy and 1 tablespoon water in a bowl set over a pan with a little simmering water in it. Remove the cake collar, and, leaving the cake on the base, place it on a plate or cake board. Trickle the icing over the top and edges, allowing it to run over. Tip a pile of Maltesers in the centre and dust them with icing sugar. Set aside in a cool place for several hours for the icing to set. I think this cake is even better the next day. It will keep well in a covered container for several days.

I'm addicted to this recipe, given to me by Tarek Malouf of the Hummingbird Bakery in London's Portobello Road. It's also the basis of the Red Velvet Bonfire Cake (page 100). Legend has it the recipe was leaked from the Waldorf-Astoria back in the 1920s.

chocolate sensation

Chocolate cream

100g dark chocolate (approx. 70% cocoa solids), broken into pieces

200ml sour cream

Cake

120g unsalted butter

300g golden caster sugar

2 large eggs

270g plain flour, sifted

230g buttermilk

1 teaspoon sea salt

1 teaspoon vanilla extract

50g cocoa powder, sifted

1 tablespoon white wine vinegar

1 teaspoon bicarbonate of soda

Chocolate icing

225g dark chocolate, broken into pieces

50g unsalted butter

2 tablespoons espresso or strong black coffee

To decorate

Chocolate shavings

4 amaretti half-dipped in chocolate

Gold or silver balls (optional)

Makes 1 x 20cm cake

To make the chocolate cream melt the chocolate in a bowl set over a pan with a little simmering water in it. Beat it into the sour cream, cover and chill for 2 hours. Preheat the oven to 170°C fan/190°C/gas mark 5 and butter two (three if you have them) 20cm sandwich or deep cake tins with a removeable base, and line the base with baking paper. Cream the butter and sugar in a food processor for 3–4 minutes until really light and fluffy. Add the eggs, one at a time, scraping down the sides of the bowl between each addition. Now add the flour in three goes, alternating with the buttermilk, beginning and ending with flour. Add the salt, vanilla extract and cocoa. Mix the vinegar and bicarbonate of soda together (it will fizz), and add to the batter. Divide the mixture between the three tins or, if using two, add a third of the mixture to each one, bake these, and then bake the third sponge once the other two are cooling. (I weigh the mixture then divide it to get evenly thick sponges.) Bake the cakes for 20–25 minutes until shrinking from the sides and firm when pressed in the centre. Leave to cool for 10 minutes then turn the cakes out onto a wire rack, remove the paper and cool the right way up.

To assemble the cake, spread one layer with half the chocolate cream, top with another layer and spread with the cream, then lay the third layer in place. For the icing, melt half the chocolate and butter in a small pan over a low heat, stirring until smooth, then stir in 1 tablespoon coffee. Spread it over the top and sides of the cake with a palette knife. Leave to set for 1 hour. Repeat with the remaining half of ingredients, this time pressing the chocolate shavings into the sides of the cake. Pile the amaretti into the centre and scatter with gold or silver balls, if using. Leave for another hour to set. Transfer the cake to a cake board or serving plate. The cake can be stored in an airtight container in the fridge for several days, in which case bring it back up to room temperature for 30 minutes before serving.

A chocolate Victoria sponge translates into a whizz-bang Black Forest Gâteau, given the speed with which the cake can be whipped up. And, considering Albert's nationality, it seems appropriate to marry it with a cake of German origin. For a really chocolatey cake, simply fill the centre with a good-quality chocolate spread.

black forest victoria

Cake

225g unsalted butter, diced
200g golden caster sugar
1 tablespoon golden syrup
200g self-raising flour
2 teaspoons baking powder
25g cocoa powder, sifted
4 medium eggs
100ml milk

Filling

300g black cherry jam
1 tablespoon kirsch
350ml double cream
2 tablespoons finely grated dark
    chocolate

Makes 1 x 20cm cake

Preheat the oven to 170°C fan/190°C/gas mark 5 and butter a 20cm cake tin 9cm deep with a removeable base. Put all the cake ingredients in a food processor and cream together. Transfer the mixture to the prepared tin, smoothing the surface and bake for 50–55 minutes or until a skewer inserted into the centre comes out clean. Run a knife around the collar of the cake and leave it to cool.

Blend the jam with the kirsch in a bowl. In another bowl, whisk the cream until it just starts to form soft peaks, but take care not to let it stiffen to a buttery consistency or it will be difficult to spread. You can leave the cake on the base or remove it as you prefer.

Slit the cake into three layers with a bread knife, and spread the lower layer with half of the jam and half of the cream. Repeat with the next layer, using up most of the remaining jam, all the cream, and lay the top layer in place. Use the last of the jam in the bowl to glaze the top of the cake with a pastry brush, then scatter over the grated chocolate. I like the cake best served freshly assembled, but it can also be chilled for up to a couple of days, in which case bring it back up to room temperature for 30–60 minutes before serving.

This is about as close as you will get to the original classy number created in the early nineteenth century by Franz Sacher, chef to Metternich. The recipe is from a favourite cookery book, *Festive Baking in Austria, Germany and Switzerland* by Sarah Kelly.

sachertorte

Cake

180g dark chocolate (approx. 70% cocoa
   solids), broken into pieces
150g unsalted butter, softened
125g icing sugar, sifted
6 large eggs, separated
125g golden caster sugar
140g plain flour, sifted twice

Glaze

350g apricot jam

Icing

300g icing sugar
225g dark chocolate, broken
   into pieces
Lightly whipped cream to serve

Makes 1 x 23cm cake

Preheat the oven to 160°C fan/180°C/gas mark 4 and butter a 23cm cake tin 9cm deep with a removeable base. Line the bottom with baking paper, butter this too and dust with flour.

Melt the chocolate for the cake in a bowl set over a pan with a little simmering water in it, stirring occasionally. Remove the bowl and allow the chocolate to cool. Cream the butter and icing sugar together in a food processor until pale. Beat in the egg yolks one at a time, then add the chocolate. Transfer to a large bowl. Whisk the egg whites until half stiff – they should hold their shape but not be dry. Add the caster sugar a tablespoon at a time, beating for about 20 seconds with each addition. Continue for 2 minutes until the meringue is glossy. Fold the meringue into the creamed mixture then fold in the flour. Transfer the mixture to the tin, smooth the surface, give it a tap on the worktop to bring up any air bubbles and bake for about 50 minutes until it is shrinking from the sides and firm in the centre, or a skewer inserted into the centre comes out clean. Turn the cake onto a wire rack, remove the paper and leave to cool the right way up.

Gently heat the jam in a small saucepan, pass through a sieve and brush the top and sides all over, then leave for a couple of hours to cool and set. To make the icing, bring the sugar, chocolate and 125ml water to the boil in a small pan. Heat to 105°C on a sugar thermometer. Stir for a minute off the heat, then drop a little onto a cold plate; the surface should set quite quickly. If it doesn't, stir for another minute. Put the cake on a rack (clingfilm underneath helps the clearing up) and pour the icing over the top to coat it, and around the edges so it runs down the sides. Avoid spreading it with a knife to preserve its glassy surface. Store the cake in a cool place overnight before serving. It keeps well for up to 5 days in an airtight container. Serve with whipped cream.

In the good old days, you had to boil up a can of condensed milk for a couple of hours to get the rich toffee-like cream that features in banoffee pie. But now you can buy dulce de leche (see page 9). Serve this delicious mousse cake lightly chilled.

chocolate and raspberry cream pie

225g dark chocolate digestive biscuits, broken

75g unsalted butter, melted

Mousse

250g dark chocolate (approx. 50% cocoa solids)

5 medium eggs, separated

200g dulce de leche or toffee spread

200g raspberries

2 tablespoons chocolate shavings

Makes 1 x 20cm cake

Whizz the chocolate biscuits to fine crumbs in a food processor. Melt the butter in a small pan and stir in the crumbs. Use the back of a spoon to press them into the base of a 20cm cake tin 9cm deep with a removeable base. Place in the fridge while making the mousse.

Put the dark chocolate in a bowl, set in a small pan over simmering water, and gently melt it. Try not to heat it much over blood temperature; if it does, leave it to cool before the next stage. Beat in the egg yolks. Whisk the egg whites in a large bowl until stiff and then fold them, in three goes, into the mixture. Smooth the dulce de leche over the biscuit base, then pour the chocolate mousse on top and smooth the surface. Cover and chill for about 1 hour until the mousse firms up a little, then top with the raspberries, then the chocolate shavings. Cover and chill for 2 hours. The cake can be made up to a couple of days in advance.

I've always loved chocolate-coated prunes, and there's a Polish deli I know in West London that does a fine trade of warding off the homesick blues for expats. It has won over the local population too.

chocolate prune cake

150g dark chocolate (approx. 50% cocoa solids), broken into pieces

225g unsalted butter, diced

225g light muscovado sugar

4 medium eggs, separated

100ml dark rum

200g ground almonds

1 teaspoon baking powder, sifted

250g stoned, no soak prunes, roughly sliced

1 tablespoon plain flour

Icing sugar for dusting

Chocolate raisins to decorate (optional)

Makes 1 x 20cm cake

Preheat the oven to 170°C fan/190°C/gas mark 5 and butter a 20cm cake tin 9cm deep with a removeable base. Put the dark chocolate in a bowl set over a small pan with a little simmering water in it, and gently melt, stirring occasionally, then set the bowl aside to cool.

Cream the butter and sugar together in a food processor until pale and fluffy. Add the egg yolks one at a time, then the rum and chocolate. Now add the ground almonds and baking powder. Transfer the mixture to a large bowl. Whisk the egg whites in a bowl and fold them into the cake mixture in two goes. Toss the sliced prunes with the flour and fold in. Transfer the mixture to the prepared tin, smoothing the surface, and bake for 60–70 minutes until a skewer inserted into the centre comes out clean. Run a knife around the collar and leave to cool.

Remove the collar, leave the cake on the base if you like. Dust the surface with icing sugar, and pile some chocolate raisins in the centre if you wish.

This is one of those rich fudgey cakes, a bit like a brownie, that can easily stand in for pud. While ground almonds are more expensive than flour they provide a delicate soft texture that is particularly good. Crème chantilly is basically French for whipped cream; it sounds nicer the way they say it.

chocolate gâteau with crème chantilly

Cake

150g dark chocolate (approx.
  50% cocoa solids), broken up
75g golden caster sugar
150g unsalted butter, diced
1 tablespoon runny honey
4 large eggs, separated
200g ground almonds
75ml milk
Cocoa powder for dusting

Crème chantilly

300ml whipping cream
40g icing sugar, sifted
2 tablespoons strong black coffee

Makes 1 x 20cm cake

Preheat the oven to 170°C fan/190°C/gas mark 5 and butter a 20cm cake tin 9cm deep with a removeable base. Place the chocolate, sugar, butter and honey in a bowl set over a pan of simmering water and gently melt, stirring frequently until everything is melted and amalgamated. Transfer to a large bowl and beat in the egg yolks and the ground almonds, then stir in the milk. Whisk the egg whites in a large bowl until they are stiff then fold them in three goes into the cake mixture. Transfer it to the prepared tin, give it several sharp taps on the worktop to bring up any air bubbles and bake for 35–40 minutes until risen and a skewer inserted into the centre comes out clean. Run a knife around the collar of the cake to loosen it and leave it to cool.

To make the crème chantilly, whisk all the ingredients in a large bowl until the cream forms soft peaks. If not serving straight away transfer it to a smaller bowl, cover and chill until required. If you leave it for longer than about 30 minutes you will need to whisk it again. Serve the cake in slices with the crème chantilly spooned on top, dusted with cocoa.

I'm not sure when Swiss Rolls turned into roulades (they're one and the same), but I quite like the retro reference that evokes childhood memories of unravelling the spiral shell of cake little by little until you reached the centre.

chocolate fudge swiss roll

Sponge

50g cocoa powder
Pinch of sea salt
3 large eggs
75g light muscovado sugar
Icing sugar

Filling

100g dark chocolate (approx. 50% cocoa solids), broken into pieces
1 tablespoon dark muscovado sugar
1 teaspoon vanilla extract
200ml whipping cream
Chocolate curls (optional)

Makes 1 x 23cm roll

Preheat the oven to 180°C fan/200°C/gas mark 5 and butter a 23cm x 32cm Swiss roll tin, line it with baking paper and butter this too. Sift the cocoa into a bowl and add the salt. Place the eggs and muscovado sugar in a bowl and whisk for 8–10 minutes with an electric whisk, until the mixture is pale and mousse-like. You can also do this in a food processor using the whisking attachment, for about 5 minutes. Lightly fold in the cocoa in two goes. Pour the mixture into the prepared tin and smooth the surface. Give the tin a couple of sharp taps on the worktop to eliminate any large bubbles and bake for 8–10 minutes until set and springy to the touch.

Lay out a clean tea towel and sift over a fine layer of icing sugar. Turn the cake out onto it and carefully roll it up with the tea towel leaving the paper in place, starting at the short end. Leave this to cool for 40-60 minutes.

For the filling, melt the chocolate with the sugar, vanilla and 2 tablespoons cream in a bowl set over a pan of simmering water, stirring until smooth, then set the bowl aside to cool. Whisk the remaining cream until it is stiff and fold in the cooled, melted chocolate.

Carefully unroll the sponge and peel off the baking paper. Spread with the chocolate cream, then roll the sponge up again and tip it onto a long serving plate, seam downwards. Dust with icing sugar, and decorate with chocolate curls if liked. Chill, uncovered, for 2 hours. If chilling longer than this, bring it back up to room temperature for 30 minutes before serving, dust it with icing sugar and decorate it at the last minute.

Clarissa Dickson Wright gave these the stamp of honour when she used to come into the café at Books for Cooks in London's Notting Hill and eat two helpings – something I'm sure she wouldn't mind me saying marks her as one of life's gourmands. This is pure chocolate truffle, soft as silk in the centre with the thinnest cakey crust around the outside.

mini chocolate mousse cakes

450g dark chocolate (approx. 50% cocoa solids), broken into pieces

125g unsalted butter

2 heaped tablespoons golden caster sugar

4 medium organic eggs

1 tablespoon plain flour, sifted

Crème fraîche to serve (optional)

Cocoa powder for dusting (optional)

Makes 8

Preheat the oven to 200°C fan/220°C/gas mark 7. Butter 8 small (150ml) coffee cups or ramekins. Place the chocolate, butter and half the sugar in a bowl set over a little simmering water in a saucepan and gently melt, stirring occasionally. Remove from the heat. Whisk the eggs with the remaining sugar in a food processor or using an electric whisk for 8–10 minutes until they have increased in volume several times and are very thick and pale, almost white. Transfer the egg mixture to a large bowl if using a food processor, fold in the flour, then very gently fold in the melted chocolate.

Spoon the mixture into the cups or ramekins, so they are three-quarters full, and cook for 5 minutes. The rim should be just set while the centre will be loose. Remove and leave the cakes to cool, then cover and leave in a cool place but not the fridge for a couple of hours. (You can leave them overnight, but they continue to firm up with time and are best eaten freshly made.) Serve them as they are, or with a spoon of crème fraîche on top, dusted with cocoa.

There are any number of occasions when you might want to call on this choccie cake, which, with no butter or cream, is everyone's best friend. It keeps well for several days in the fridge, the liquid in the ricotta seeps into the sponge and keeps it moist.

guilt-free chocolate cake

Sponge

4 medium eggs, separated
150g golden caster sugar
3 tablespoons cocoa powder, sifted
225g ground almonds
1 teaspoon baking powder, sifted

Filling

2 x 250g tubs of ricotta, drained
3 tablespoons set honey
4 tablespoons coarsely grated dark
    chocolate (70–85% cocoa solids)

Makes 1 x 20cm cake

Preheat the oven to 180°C fan/200°C/gas mark 6 and butter a 20cm cake tin 9cm deep with a removeable base. Stiffly whisk the egg whites in a medium bowl – I use a handheld electric whisk for this. Whisk together the egg yolks and sugar in a large bowl until pale and creamy. Fold the egg whites into the egg mixture in three goes, then fold in the cocoa, the ground almonds and baking powder. Transfer the cake mixture to the prepared tin, smooth the surface and bake it for 35 minutes until the sponge has begun to shrink from the sides and a skewer inserted into the centre comes out clean. Run a knife around the edge of the cake and leave it to cool in the tin.

Place the ricotta and honey in a food processor and whizz until smooth (if you do this by hand it will remain grainy). Remove the collar from the cake, but you can leave it on the base for ease of serving. Slit the cake in half, taking into account the height in the centre of the cake. Reserving a couple of tablespoons of the ricotta cream, spread the rest over the base and sandwich with the top half. Spread the reserved cream in a thin layer over the surface of the cake and scatter over the grated chocolate which should conceal all but the very edge of the cream. Set aside in a cool place. If keeping the cake longer than a few hours, cover, chill and bring it back up to room temperature for 30–60 minutes before serving.

meringues and patisserie

Meringues are really very simple, for all their heart-stopping beauty or resemblance to movie special effects. Professional ones have local identities: Italian meringues require their cook to stand by with thermometer in hand to catch the sugar syrup at an exact temperature, which is why my staple meringue recipe is French. It needs only a whisk and a bowl. I like the simple life. (There are also Swiss meringues, and even exquisite Japanese ones, but let's not go there.)

I've also included in this section, which covers the kind of goodies you would expect to buy over the marble counter and take home carefully in a large white box, those wonderful French tarts that can be eaten with morning coffee, afternoon tea, or as a dessert after any meal – fruit and custard in a pastry case. They're glamorous all-rounders. There are also streusels, from the German (*streuen* meaning to sprinkle or scatter), which actually combine the best of French and British traditions – a crumble on a fruit tart base. Good with all kinds of fruits – plums, apples, pears as well as the berries and figs here. See what's really ripe on the stall or in the greengrocer and work from there.

In essence meringues are all variations on the theme of a froth of sugar and egg whites; from there it is down to how you bake them, depending on whether you want them crisp and melting, or gooey inside for dunking into jammy compôtes and smearing with cream. But first, a few pointers for success. Of all the cakes in this book meringues are the most likely to cause problems, and it's worth reading the small print before you start.

meringue essentials

the egg whites

The eggs should be at room temperature, so if you normally keep them in the fridge remember to take them out 1 hour or so beforehand to warm up.

In addition be sure they are either organic or free range. Poor quality battery-produced eggs will have watery whites that fail to rise.

the sugar

Meringues conform to a basic ratio of 1 large egg white to around 50g sugar. This is the same whether you are making crunchy individual meringues, layers, nests or a pavlova. What differs and creates the various types is how you bake them.

While I normally advocate unrefined sugar in recipes, I prefer to use refined caster sugar for meringues to encourage that snowy white hue, unless of course you fancy a brown sugar meringue, which is delicious too, if altogether different. I either use caster sugar, or half caster and half icing sugar.

enemies

Meringues have two arch enemies. The first is water, and even a drop in the bowl or on the whisk will prevent the whites from rising. The other is grease – including even the tiniest bit of yolk. It is essential that your bowl and whisk are scrupulously clean.

utensils

The bowl should be nice and big, but not with such a large base area that the white is too shallow to whip effectively. Large pudding and old-fashioned ceramic mixing bowls are ideal.

As to the whisk, a hand-held electric one will speed you through the process.

master recipe

3 large egg whites, at room temperature
175g caster sugar

Makes 6 medium meringues

Preheat the oven to 120°C fan/140°C/gas mark 1. Put the egg whites in a large bowl and whisk them until they rise into a froth the consistency of shaving foam. Sprinkle over 1 heaped tablespoon sugar at a time, whisking well with each addition until you have a smooth, glossy meringue. You can increase the sugar to 2 tablespoons towards the end. In theory the meringue should be stiff enough for you to invert the bowl, though I prefer not to risk this.

Line one or two baking trays with baking paper. You can dab a little meringue mixture onto the corners of the trays to glue the paper down. Drop heaped tablespoons of the mixture onto the paper, leaving plenty of space between each one. You can make them bigger than this: a handful of large blowsy meringues placed centrally on the table for people to break up and help themselves makes for informal eating. Alternatively, if they are destined to be sandwiched together for tea you can make them smaller, in which case reduce the cooking time accordingly.

Put the meringues in the oven and turn it down to 100°C fan/120°C/gas mark 1/2. Cook for 2 hours and, if you are using two trays, switch them around halfway through. After this time the meringues should be crisp on the outside, and fluffy within; if you tap the base it should sound hollow. For a gooier meringue, bake for 2–2 1/2 hours at 120°C fan/140°C/gas mark 1. Remove and leave them to cool. They can be stored in an airtight container for 2 weeks.

variations

Chocolate Stir 1 heaped tablespoon sifted cocoa into the finished meringue mixture. Delicious with butterscotch ice-cream, chocolate sauce and toasted flaked almonds.

Almond Scatter flaked almonds over the meringues before baking them and dust with icing sugar to serve. Good with vanilla custard and poached fruit, e.g. rhubarb and plums.

Hazelnut Scatter a few chopped hazelnuts over the meringues before baking them. Good for serving with caramelised apples and pears, and whipped cream.

Pistachio Sprinkle a few chopped pistachios over the meringues before baking. Serve with raspberries and blackberries, pears in red wine, chocolate and coffee creams, or lemon and orange sorbet.

Brown sugar Use light muscovado sugar and bake the meringues for 2 hours at 120°C fan/140°C/gas mark 1.

filling the meringues

• Dip the base of small meringues into melted dark chocolate and sandwich together.
• Flavour softly whipped cream with coffee, chocolate or vanilla.
• Almost any fruit goes beautifully with meringues, its natural tartness perfectly offsetting all that sugar.
• Meringues with ice-cream is not only instant but sufficiently glam to round off the best of suppers.
• Try a mascarpone filling (see page 35) instead of cream.

This is an old favourite of mine, a meringue cake that is crisp on the outside and moussey within, studded with hidden treasures. You can use almost any combination of dried fruits and nuts that takes your fancy. I'd serve it with a plain vanilla or rich chocolate ice-cream, otherwise a spicy one such as cinnamon or nutmeg.

ginger, almond and fig meringue

110g whole almonds, blanched and coarsely chopped

4 large egg whites, at room temperature

225g caster sugar

150g dried figs, coarsely chopped

75g preserved ginger, coarsely chopped

Makes 1 x 20cm cake

Preheat the oven to 170°C fan/190°C/gas mark 5. Lay the almonds on a baking tray and toast for 10 minutes. Whisk the egg whites in a bowl until they rise into a foam, then gradually whisk in the sugar a tablespoon or two at a time, whisking well with each addition until you have a stiff, glossy meringue. Fold in the almonds, figs and ginger. Spoon the mixture into a 20cm cake tin 9cm deep with a removeable base and bake for 35 minutes until a skewer inserted into the centre comes out clean. Run a knife around the collar and leave the cake to cool. Ideally it should be eaten on the day it is made.

I couldn't help but look drily at the emergence of lemon tart as the darling of fashionable menus during the 1980s; in my eyes it wasn't a patch on my mother's lemon meringue pie. We tend to be a bit sniffy about ingredients like digestive biscuits and condensed milk these days, but they're great pudding staples and make life easy. Lemon meringue pies have a habit of oozing sticky syrup – something I like, so no attempt has been made here to change the habit.

lemon meringue pie

225g digestive biscuits, broken
110g unsalted butter, melted
Finely grated zest and juice
   of 4 lemons
1 x 400g tin condensed milk
4 large eggs, at room
   temperature, separated
110g caster sugar

Makes 1 x 20cm pie

Whizz the biscuits to fine crumbs in a food processor. Put the crumbs in a bowl, add the melted butter and toss until the crumbs are evenly coated. Press the mixture onto the sides and base of a 20cm cake tin 9cm deep with a removeable base. Start with the sides and then do the base, using your fingers to press the mixture down.

Preheat the oven to 170°C fan/190°C/gas mark 5. Before juicing the lemons, roll them on the worktop to release as much juice as possible. Combine the zest and juice with the condensed milk in a bowl, whisking until you have a smooth cream. Now whisk in the egg yolks and pour on top of the biscuit crust. Whisk the egg whites in a large bowl until they rise to a froth. Sprinkle over the sugar 1 tablespoon at a time, whisking well with each addition until you have a glossy, stiff meringue. (This is less sugar than you would normally use for a meringue, to account for the sweetness of the base.)

Mound the meringue mixture on top of the lemon cream, taking it to the edge of the tin. Bake for 30 minutes or until the surface of the meringue is lightly golden and crusty, and the custard set. Remove from the oven, and leave to cool. Run a knife around the collar to loosen the sides and remove the collar. The pie is at its best eaten the day it is made. If you do chill it, then bring it back up to room temperature before serving.

Just hard enough on the outside to hold their shape. You can nibble on these with a coffee, or serve them with ice-cream or some fruit as suggested.

pistachio choc-chip meringues

4 large egg whites, at room temperature

250g caster sugar

50g dark chocolate chips, or chopped dark chocolate

50g chopped pistachios

350g raspberries

6 passionfruit, halved

Crème fraîche to serve

Makes 6 large hearts

Preheat the oven to 120°C fan/140°C/gas mark 1. Put the egg whites in a large bowl and whisk them until they rise to a froth. Sprinkle over 1 heaped tablespoon of sugar at a time, whisking well with each addition until you have a smooth, glossy meringue. You can increase the sugar to 2 tablespoons towards the end.

Line one or two baking trays with baking paper. Fold the chocolate chips and two-thirds of the nuts into the meringue. For each meringue drop 3 heaped tablespoons of the mixture onto the paper in the shape of a triangle, then using a table knife smooth this into a heart shape. Leave plenty of space between each one. Scatter over the remaining pistachios.

Place the meringues in the oven and turn it down to 110°C fan/130°C/gas mark $1/2$. Cook for 2 hours; it is not a bad idea to switch the trays around halfway through, but don't worry if you forget. By this time the meringues should be crisp on the outside, and if you tap the base it should sound hollow within. Remove and leave them to cool. They can be stored in an airtight container for 2 weeks.

Serve them with a pile of raspberries and the passionfruit seeds spooned over, and a spoon of crème fraîche.

red berry pavlova

Snowy white meringue and blood red strawberries look deliciously dramatic. Within your choice of red fruits, I'd lean heavily towards raspberries, and, if you can get them, some loganberries and wild strawberries for a real treat.

Pavlova

6 large egg whites, at
room temperature

350g caster sugar

1 tablespoon cornflour

1 teaspoon white wine
vinegar

Red berry sauce

800g red berries, hulled

40g icing sugar

2 tablespoons raspberry
eau-de-vie or kirsch
(optional)

Squeeze of lemon juice

300ml whipping cream

Makes 1 x 20cm cake

Preheat the oven to 200°C fan/220°C/gas mark 7. Cut a circle of baking paper to fit a 20cm cake tin 9cm deep with a removeable base. Rinse the tin with water, put the paper circle on the base and rinse it again.

Whisk the egg whites in a bowl until they rise to a froth. Sprinkle over the caster sugar a few tablespoons at a time, whisking well with each addition. Whisk in the cornflour, then the vinegar. You should have a very stiff, glossy meringue.

Spoon the meringue into the prepared tin and smooth the surface. Place the pavlova on a baking sheet in the oven, reduce the temperature to its very lowest setting and bake for $1^1/_2$–2 hours keeping an eye on the surface to make sure it doesn't colour. Remove the pavlova and run a knife around the edge of the tin.

Put a third of the berries, the icing sugar, the eau-de-vie if using, and the lemon juice in a liquidiser and purée. Pass through a sieve into a bowl, taste and add more sugar or lemon juice as necessary. Halve or quarter any large strawberries and mix the remaining fruit in with the sauce.

Remove the collar and transfer the pavlova to a large serving plate. Whip the cream and spread thickly over the top of the pavlova. Spoon the berries and sauce into the centre with extra around the base if liked. Serve straight away.

A streusel sports crumble on top and shortbread underneath – this one comes with the charm of a summer pudding with redcurrants and raspberries in between. In the same vein, some whipped or clotted cream would go down a treat.

redcurrant and raspberry streusel

200g plain flour

110g ground almonds

110g caster sugar

225g unsalted butter, chilled and diced

40g flaked almonds

40g pine nuts

200g redcurrants

250g raspberries

100g raspberry jam

Makes 1 x 20cm cake

Preheat the oven to 170°C fan/190°C/gas mark 5. Put the flour, ground almonds and caster sugar in a food processor. Add the butter and reduce the mixture to crumbs (it's very important that the butter is cold otherwise it will cream into a dough). As it starts to resemble a crumble, transfer half the mixture to a bowl and toss in the flaked almonds and pine nuts.

Continue to process the remaining mixture until it forms a smooth pastry dough. Using your fingers, press this into the base of a 20cm cake tin 9cm deep with a removeable base. String the redcurrants into a bowl using a fork, add the raspberries and the jam and gently mix together. Spoon the fruit over the shortbread base. Scatter the crumble and nut mixture over the top of the fruit and bake for 45 minutes until the top is golden and crisp and the juices are bubbling. Remove and allow the tart to cool, then run a knife around the collar and serve.

Figs, almonds and honey topped with a dollop of yogurt are the stuff Greek islands are made of. And while we're dreaming, one of those powdery black coffees laced with cardamom and lots of sugar would be great.

fig streusel

200g plain flour
110g ground almonds
110g golden caster sugar
225g unsalted butter,
   chilled and diced

500g figs, stalks trimmed,
   and cut into quarters
2 tablespoons runny honey
40g flaked almonds
Icing sugar for dusting

Makes approx. 12

Preheat the oven to 170°C fan/190°C/gas mark 5. Put the flour, ground almonds and caster sugar in a food processor. Add the butter and reduce the mixture to crumbs (it's very important that the butter is cold otherwise it will cream into a dough). As it starts to resemble a crumble, transfer the mixture to a bowl. Scatter half the crumble mixture over the bottom of a 30 x 23 x 4cm non-stick traybake tin and, using your fingers, press it onto the base. Scatter over the fig quarters and then drizzle with the honey. Stir the flaked almonds into the remaining crumble mixture and scatter this over the top. There should be tips of fruit showing through.

Bake for 45 minutes until the top is golden and crisp. Remove and allow the traybake to cool, then dust the surface with icing sugar. Run a knife around the edge of the tin and cut the streusel into squares.

Pastry

60g unsalted butter, softened

60g golden caster sugar

$1/2$ medium egg

125g plain flour, sifted

15g ground almonds

Filling

70g unsalted butter, softened

100g golden caster sugar

100g ground almonds

1 medium egg, plus 1 egg white

1 large apple (or $1^{1}/4$ average-size),
   peeled, quartered, cored and sliced

Icing sugar for dusting

Makes 1 x 23cm tart

This classic apple tart is a personal favourite: sliced apples
cushioned by a buttery almond sponge with crisp pastry below.

apple and almond tart

To make the pastry, cream the butter and sugar together in a food processor. Mix in the egg, then add the flour and ground almonds. As soon as the dough begins to form a ball, wrap it in clingfilm and chill for at least 2 hours; it can be kept in the fridge for several days until you are ready to use it.

Preheat the oven to 170°C fan/190°C/gas mark 5. Thinly roll out the pastry on a lightly floured surface and line the bottom and sides of a 23 x 3 cm tart tin with a removeable base, trimming the excess. (Don't worry if it tears and you end up partly pressing it into the tin.) Line the case with baking paper and fill it with baking beans or a dried pulse. Cook for 15–20 minutes until starting to colour at the sides, then remove the paper and beans and leave to cool.

To make the filling, put the butter, sugar and ground almonds in a food processor and blend together, then add the egg and egg white and mix to a smooth cream. Smooth this over the base of the pastry case. Arrange the apple slices on top and bake for 30–40 minutes or until golden, risen and firm. Leave to cool and then dust with icing sugar.

fig custard tart

To make the pastry, cream the butter and sugar together in a food processor until soft and fluffy. Add the egg yolk and process until well combined, then gradually add the flour and ground almonds and bring the dough together with a drop of milk. Wrap the pastry in clingfilm and chill for at least 2 hours; it will keep for several days.

Preheat the oven to 180°C fan/200°C/gas mark 6. Allow the dough to come to room temperature for a few minutes, and then knead until pliable. Roll out the dough on a lightly floured worktop to about 2mm thick, and use it to line the base and sides of a 23cm tart tin 3cm deep with a removeable base. Run a rolling pin over the top to trim the excess pastry and reserve the trimmings to patch the case once it is cooked. The pastry is quite fragile so don't worry if you end up partly pressing it into the tin. Line the case with tin foil, tucking it over the top edge, fill it with baking beans or a dried pulse and bake for 15 minutes. Remove the foil and baking beans; if any part of the side has shrunk more than it should, patch it with the reserved pastry. Brush the inside of the case with the egg white and bake for a further 10 minutes until lightly golden. Leave the case to cool. Again you can patch any cracks that might have appeared before filling it.

Place the tart case on a baking tray to make it easier to transfer to and from the oven. Slice each fig into three, cutting downwards. Whisk the cream with the egg, egg yolks, 50g of the caster sugar and the amaretto. Pour the mixture into the tart case. Settle the figs on the surface of the custard and sprinkle the remaining caster sugar over them. Bake for 30–35 minutes until the custard is set and golden on the surface. Remove and leave the tart to cool.

Pastry

75g unsalted butter, softened
75g golden caster sugar
1 medium egg, separated
200g plain flour
20g ground almonds
Milk

Filling

5 figs, stalks trimmed
300ml whipping cream
1 medium egg, and 2 egg yolks
50g golden caster sugar, plus 1 teaspoon
1 tablespoon amaretto or other liqueur

Makes 1 x 23cm tart

Pastry

200g plain flour
30g golden caster suar
100g unsalted butter, diced
1 medium egg yolk

Custard

9 medium eggs
300g golden caster sugar
Finely grated zest and juice of
   2 lemons
Finely grated zest and juice of
   2 oranges
250ml double cream
Icing sugar for dusting

Makes 1 x 20cm tart

A tart of the deep custard variety, while orange
combined with lemon produces a perfect balance.

lemon
and orange
custard tart

To prepare the pastry, put the flour, sugar and butter in a food processor, and
reduce to a crumb-like consistency. Add the egg yolk and enough water to bring
the dough together into a ball. Reserve a small amount of the pastry to patch any
cracks once the case is cooked and, using your fingers, press the remainder into a
20cm cake tin 9cm deep with a removeable base so the pastry comes about 6cm
up the sides (butter and flour the tin first if it isn't non-stick). Chill it for 1 hour.

Preheat the oven to 180°C fan/200°C/gas mark 6. Line the pastry case with tin foil
and baking beans or a dried pulse, securing the pastry sides firmly to the tin, and
bake it for 15 minutes until the pastry has set. Remove the foil and beans and
bake for a further 10–15 minutes until lightly golden and fully baked. Allow it to
cool, then patch any cracks that have appeared with the reserved pastry.

Lower the oven temperature to 130°C fan/150°C/gas mark 2. Whisk together the
eggs and sugar in a large bowl, then whisk in the lemon and orange juice and zest
and the cream. Pour the mixture into the pastry shell set on a baking sheet and
bake for $1^1/2$ hours until set. Check after 45 minutes to make sure it is starting to
set, and turn the heat up if it is still a barely warm liquid, down if it seems to be
cooking too fast. Remove the tart from the oven as soon as it has set and leave to
cool to room temperature. Trim the top of the pastry level with the custard, leaving
the collar of the tin in place. Cover and chill the tart for several hours, and remove
30 minutes before eating. Dust the surface with icing sugar just before serving.

cheesecakes

Cheesecakes can make or break reputations. Damon Runyan – who wrote fabulously about New York, as in his tale that became the musical *Guys and Dolls* – used to begin stories with, 'I was sitting in Mindy's, partaking of some cheesecake...' Everybody knew what he meant. Mindy's was a café famed for its cheesecake – you went there to have it, you would have fought your way there to have it, you dreamed of it when far away from Manhattan. It would have been a classic cheesecake that had evolved in melting-pot cuisine – baked, set with raisins, or just possibly lemon, or a chilled strawberry affair. It seemed simple, but it took daily Big Apple know-how to get it exactly right every time.

The best cheesecakes are simultaneously firm and creamy. And that isn't always easy: depending on whether they're made with cream cheese, ricotta, double or even clotted cream, you have to add just the right amount of egg (or with chilled cheesecake, gelatine), to make sure that they set. Then comes the un-American activity: you wait while the cheesecake firms as it cools and matures overnight, until reaching perfect consistency. Since Americans are such supremos, I've also included a recipe from California which shouldn't disappoint.

Cheesecake and fruit are great bedfellows, but not the gloop of tinned pineapple or black cherries that so often features. This one, with blackcurrants and raspberries spooned over it, is much lighter than the norm – contrary to its texture ricotta has about half the calories of cream cheese.

ricotta and amaretti cheesecake

Pastry

40g unsalted butter, softened
40g caster sugar
1 large egg yolk
100g plain flour, sifted

Almond cream

100g amaretti
40g unsalted butter, diced
1 large egg

Filling

3 x 250g tubs of ricotta
225g caster sugar
40g cornflour, sifted
4 medium organic eggs
2 teaspoons vanilla extract
150g fromage frais

250g blackcurrants, removed
   from the vine
200g raspberries

Makes 1 x 20cm cheesecake

To make the pastry, cream the butter and sugar together in a food processor until light and fluffy. Beat in the egg yolk, and then add the flour. As soon as the dough begins to form a ball, wrap it in clingfilm and chill for at least 1 hour. You may need to add a couple of drops of water to bring the dough together.

Preheat the oven to 180°C fan/200°C/gas mark 6. To make the almond cream, place the amaretti in a food processor and reduce to fine crumbs – almost a powder. Add the butter and blend it with the amaretti, then beat in the egg.

Butter the base of a 20cm cake tin 9cm deep with a removeable base. On a lightly floured surface roll out the dough to about 23cm diameter and cut a circle to fit the base of the tin. Press gently into the tin. Spread the almond cream over the pastry and bake for 20 minutes until golden and firm. Remove and allow to cool. Reduce the oven temperature to 170°C fan/190°C/gas mark 5.

To make the filling, blend the ricotta with 175g sugar and the cornflour in a food processor for a couple of minutes until very creamy. Now add the eggs, one at a time, the vanilla extract and fromage frais.

Wrap foil around the tin. Pour in the mixture and smooth the surface. Place it in a roasting tray with enough hot but not boiling water to come 2cm up the sides of the tin. Bake for 1$1/2$ hours until the centre has set and the top is golden. It may wobble a little if moved from side to side, but should not appear sloppy beneath the surface. Once cooked, run a knife around the collar, remove it and allow to cool completely. Cover with clingfilm and chill for several hours, or overnight, to allow it to set to the perfect consistency.

Meanwhile, put the blackcurrants and remaining sugar in a small saucepan and gently heat for a few minutes, stirring occasionally, until the sugar has melted and the currants are almost submerged in juice. Transfer to a bowl and leave to cool, then stir in the raspberries. You can also prepare the fruit in advance and cover and chill it. Bring back up to room temperature before serving.

Remove the cheesecake from the fridge about 20 minutes before eating, and serve with the fruit spooned over.

My brothers and I grew up on this one, long before the fashion for 'lemon tarts', it worked its sharp magic. It's blissfully easy to prepare, with that retro touch of a digestive crust, so apt in a cheesecake.

my mum's lemon cheesecake

Base

150g digestive biscuits, broken
50g unsalted butter, melted

Filling

350g full-fat cream cheese
150g golden caster sugar
4 medium eggs
Finely grated zest and juice
    of 2 lemons
1 teaspoon vanilla extract
300ml sour cream

Makes 1 x 20cm cheesecake

Preheat the oven to 180°C fan/200°C/gas mark 6. Whizz the biscuits to crumbs in a food processor, add to the pan of melted butter and toss until evenly coated. Press the mixture onto the base of a 20cm cake tin 9cm deep with a removeable collar, using your fingers or the bottom of a tumbler to press the mixture down.

Place all the ingredients for the filling except the sour cream in the bowl of a food processor and whizz until smooth. Carefully pour the mixture on top of the biscuit-crumb base (I use the back of a spoon as a chute to avoid disturbing the crumbs). Bake the cheesecake for 30 minutes until it is just set and slightly risen – it may also be starting to colour. Remove and leave it for 5–10 minutes for the surface to level, then smooth the sour cream over the surface and return to the oven for 10 minutes. It may still appear slightly shiny and liquid but should firm up on cooling and chilling.

Remove and leave the cheesecake to cool, then cover it with clingfilm and chill overnight. Serve the cheesecake chilled.

This is the classic cheesecake, the one which, judging by its ubiquity, we prize above all others. And, at its best, it is small wonder – soft, creamy and set with raisins, begging for a double espresso alongside.

old-fashioned baked cheesecake

Base

25g unsalted butter, softened
25g fresh white breadcrumbs
1 teaspoon golden caster sugar

Filling

700g full-fat cream cheese
225g golden caster sugar
2 medium eggs
350ml whipping cream
40g plain flour, sifted
$1^{1}/_{2}$ teaspoons vanilla extract
75g raisins
Freshly grated nutmeg

Makes 1 x 20cm cheesecake

Preheat the oven to 180°C fan/200°C/gas mark 6 and grease a 20cm cake tin 9cm deep with a removeable base using all the butter. Mix the breadcrumbs with the sugar and press onto the sides and base of the tin.

To make the filling, blend the cream cheese and sugar in a food processor. Add the eggs and cream, then fold in the flour and the vanilla extract. With the motor off, stir in the raisins. Carefully spoon the mixture into the tin, evenly distributing the raisins. Liberally dust the surface with freshly grated nutmeg. Bake in the oven for 45 minutes until puffy around the edges and just set; it should wobble if you move it from side to side. Turn the oven off, leave the door ajar (or prop it open using a wooden spoon) and leave the cheesecake for 1 hour. Remove the cheesecake and leave to cool completely. Loosely cover with foil and chill overnight. Bring back up to room temperature for 30 minutes or so before serving.

This cheesecake is readily dressed up for pud with a dollop of a coarse apple compôte. Simmer 900g Bramley apples with the juice of $^{1}/_{2}$ lemon and 125g caster sugar, covered, for 20 minutes and then mash. Serve at room temperature.

Of many recipes I returned from California with some years back, this is the one I most frequently revisit. The cornmeal touches on the area's heritage, while the treacle and spices give the cream a hint of butterscotch.

californian cheesecake

Crust

85g plain flour, sifted
40g fine polenta or cornmeal
50g golden caster sugar
85g unsalted butter, melted

Filling

550g low-fat cream cheese
150ml sour cream
180g golden caster sugar
3 medium eggs
Few drops vanilla extract
$1/2$ teaspoon ground ginger
$1/2$ teaspoon ground cinnamon
1 heaped teaspoon black treacle
Cocoa powder for dusting

Makes 1 x 20cm cheesecake

Preheat the oven to 150°C fan/170°C/gas mark 3. Mix the ingredients for the crust together in a bowl and, using your fingers, press the mixture onto the bottom of a 20cm cake tin 9cm deep with a removeable base. Bake for 35 minutes until pale gold, then allow to cool.

To prepare the filling, put all the ingredients listed except the cocoa in a food processor and blend until really smooth, scraping down the sides to make sure all the treacle is incorporated. Strain the mixture into the tin on top of the crust and bake for 50 minutes. The very centre of the filling should quiver when gently shaken – it will set more firmly as it cools. Run a knife around the edge of the tin to prevent the filling cracking and leave to cool completely. Loosely cover with foil and chill overnight. Serve the cheesecake chilled, remove the collar and dust liberally with cocoa.

Anyone with a penchant for poppyseed bloomers
will be able to relate to the charm of this one.
Soft and creamy with the thinnest crust, and a
fine smattering of dust-grey poppyseeds on top.
I'd pop a bottle of vodka in the freezer and serve
little shots alongside.

poppyseed cheesecake
with vodka sultanas

Put the sultanas in a bowl, pour over the vodka and leave to soak overnight.

Preheat the oven to 180°C fan/200°C/gas mark 6. To prepare the base, grease
a 20cm cake tin 9cm deep with a removeable base using all the butter. Mix
the breadcrumbs with the sugar and press to the sides and base of the tin.

To make the filling, blend the cream cheese and sugar in a food processor.
Add the eggs and cream, then fold in the flour and vanilla extract. Mix in the
sultanas and any residual liquor from soaking them. Carefully spoon the
mixture into the tin. Dust the surface with poppyseeds so it is lightly covered
with a thin layer. Bake in the oven for 45 minutes until puffy around the edges
and just set: it should wobble if you move it from side to side. Turn the oven
off, leave the door ajar (or prop it open using a wooden spoon) and leave the
cheesecake for 1 hour. Remove the cheesecake and allow it to cool completely.
It is at its best a day later, eaten at room temperature. If you chill it, then
bring it back up to room temperature 30 minutes before serving.

Base

25g unsalted butter, softened
25g fresh white breadcrumbs
1 teaspoon caster sugar

Filling

50g sultanas
4 tablespoons lemon- or other flavoured vodka
700g full-fat cream cheese
225g caster sugar
2 medium eggs
350ml whipping cream
40g plain flour, sifted
1$^{1}/_{2}$ teaspoons vanilla extract
1–2 tablespoons poppyseeds

Makes 1 x 20cm cheesecake

Midnight fridge-sneaking has everything to do with dolloping a teaspoon of clotted cream onto a square of chilled dark chocolate, or onto a gingernut, a sentiment reiterated here.

In the absence of fresh berries during the winter months, or at least ones worth eating, jams are an excellent reminder of the fruit – sweet and intense, they take minutes to whisk into a sauce for pouring over a cheesecake for pudding. You could also stir in a drop of liqueur – brandy, cointreau or a fruit eau-de-vie.

mini strawberry clotted cream cheesecakes

100g gingernuts, broken
40g unsalted butter, melted

Filling
2 sheets (6g) leaf gelatine
    or $1/2$ x 11g sachet
200g low-fat cream cheese
100g golden caster sugar
$1/2$ teaspoon vanilla extract
200g clotted cream

Sauce
250g strawberry jam
2 tablespoons lemon juice

Makes 6

Whizz the gingernuts to crumbs in a food processor. Combine with the melted butter and stir to coat them. Divide the crumbs between 6 x 9cm (150ml) ramekins, and press them into the base to form the crust.

If using gelatine sheets, cut them into wide strips and soak them in a small bowl of cold water for 5 minutes. Drain off the water, pour over another 2 tablespoons water, submerging the sheets, and stand the bowl in a second bowl of boiling water. Stir for a few minutes until the gelatine dissolves. If using the powdered form, sprinkle it on 2–3 tablespoons boiling water in a small bowl, leave for 3–4 minutes then stir to dissolve. If it has not completely dissolved, stand the bowl in another bowl of just-boiled water for a few minutes, then stir again.

Put the cream cheese in a small saucepan with the sugar and gently heat, stirring constantly with a wooden spoon until the mixture liquefies, and the sugar has dissolved. Give the mixture a quick whisk to get rid of any lumps. It should be warm – the same temperature as the gelatine solution. Beat the gelatine into the cream cheese mixture, and the vanilla extract, then transfer it to a bowl and leave to cool.

Add the clotted cream to the cooled cream cheese mixture and whisk together. You don't have to worry about the last few tiny little dots of cream blending in. Divide the mixture between the ramekins. Cover with clingfilm and chill overnight.

To prepare the strawberry sauce gently heat the jam in a small saucepan until it liquefies, then pass it through a sieve into a bowl. Stir in the lemon juice and leave to cool completely, then cover and set aside until ready to use.

Remove the cheesecakes from the fridge about 10 minutes before serving to let the crust soften just a little. Spoon some of the strawberry sauce on top of each one.

other
teatime treats

The well-dressed tea table has a complete wardrobe of goodies to chose from. They don't have to include a major investment in a single couture cake. And they don't have to be prepared a season in advance: you can swiftly improvise scones, muffins, pancakes and a trayful of aptly-named Paradise Slices if you have to, and they have a lovely home-spun charm. Accessorize with a proper teapot, good, plain china (rather than the kind kept behind glass for Sunday best), a cakestand and a posy of old-fashioned flowers.

The simplicity of this is what counts, and your willingness to put time into making it delights people, especially unexpected guests. Just laying a few full plates on the table (perhaps including a home-made biscuit or two let out of its tin) for an impromptu meal means a lot, whether for your kids' friends after school, or to say thank you to the nice man who fought your washing machine all morning. With home-made goodies, you offer something money can't buy even at the smartest cake shop: food that's personal to both the maker and the eater. Remember what people like and make it for them. Can't beat that.

French buttercream can be eaten with abandon compared to the traditional version: it is lighter and less sweet, consisting of about two-thirds custard. These make great mini birthday cakes stuck with a candle.

iced fancies

Sponge

3 large eggs

75g golden caster sugar

50g plain flour, sifted

Pinch of sea salt

Buttercream

3 medium eggs

150g icing sugar, sifted

50g plain flour, sifted

325ml full-fat milk

Finely grated zest of 1/2 lemon

1/2 teaspoon vanilla extract

180g unsalted butter, softened

Icing

225g icing sugar, sifted

2–3 tablespoons lemon juice, sieved

Blue and yellow food colouring, paste or liquid

White writing icing

Mini-marshmallows (ideally pink and yellow) to decorate

Makes 12

To make the sponge, preheat the oven to 180°C fan/200°C/gas mark 6. Butter a 23 x 32 x 4cm Swiss roll tin, line it with baking paper and butter this also. Put the eggs and sugar in a bowl and whisk for 8–10 minutes using a hand-held electric whisk, until the mixture is almost white and mousse-like (or you can do this in a food processor using the whisking attachment, for about 5 minutes). Lightly fold in the flour in two goes, then the salt. Pour the mixture into the prepared tin and smooth it using a palette knife. Give the tin a couple of sharp taps on the worktop to eliminate any large bubbles and bake the sponge for 8–10 minutes until it is lightly golden and springy to the touch. Run a knife around the edge of the cake and leave it to cool.

To make the buttercream, first whisk the eggs and icing sugar together in a medium non-stick saucepan until smooth, and then whisk in the flour. Bring the milk to the boil in a small pan, and whisk it into the egg mixture. Return the mixture to a low heat and cook for a few minutes until the custard thickens, stirring vigorously with a wooden spoon to disperse any lumps that form. The custard shouldn't actually boil, but the odd bubble will ensure it is hot enough to thicken properly. Cook for a few more minutes, stirring constantly. Pass the custard through a sieve into a bowl, stir in the lemon zest and vanilla, cover the surface with clingfilm and leave to cool completely.

Beat the softened butter in a bowl until light and creamy. If it's still on the hard side, cream it in a food processor and then transfer it to a bowl. Using a hand-held electric whisk, gradually whisk in the cooled custard, then whisk for a few more minutes, initially on a low speed then on a higher speed, until it is very pale and fluffy.

Turn the cake onto a board and peel off the paper. Cut it in half widthways. Line a plate or dish with clingfilm to assemble the cake. Thickly spread buttercream over one half, right up the edge, then sandwich with the other half, smoothing the edges of the buttercream level with the cake. Loosely cover with clingfilm and chill for a couple of hours.

Slice the cake into 12 cubes approx. 4cm. Blend the icing sugar with enough lemon juice to thickly coat the cake and trickle down the sides. Transfer half the icing to another bowl and tint each batch a pastel shade, one with a tiny bit of blue food colouring, the other with yellow. Ice the surface of half the cubes with blue icing and the rest with yellow, taking it up to the edge of the cake. Allow the icing to trickle down the sides for a few minutes, and then decorate the top with a zigzag of writing icing, and a few marshmallows. Set aside in a cool place to set for 1 hour. Cover and chill if not serving immediately.

As if proof were needed that the simplest is the best, this recipe relies on a minimum of fuss, just the divine marriage of lemon, butter and the crunch of sugar. The sponge itself is meltingly tender and fluffy.

lemon drizzle traybake

225g unsalted butter, diced
225g golden caster sugar
3 medium eggs
150ml milk
225g self-raising flour, sifted
1¹/₂ teaspoons baking powder, sifted
Finely grated zest and juice of 2 lemons
100g golden granulated sugar

Makes 1 x 30 x 23cm traybake

Preheat the oven to 170°C fan oven/190°C/gas mark 5 and butter a 30 x 23 x 4cm baking tin. Put the butter and caster sugar in a food processor and beat together until pale and fluffy. Incorporate the eggs, one at a time, scraping down the sides of the bowl if necessary, then add the milk and whizz until creamy. Gradually add the flour and baking powder through the funnel with the motor running, then incorporate the lemon zest.

Transfer the mixture to the prepared tin, smoothing the surface and bake for 30 minutes until golden and shrinking slightly from the sides, or a skewer comes out clean from the centre.

Run a knife around the edge of the tin and prick the cake with a skewer at about 2cm intervals. Combine the lemon juice and granulated sugar in a bowl, stirring to evenly distribute it, then spoon over the top of the cake. Leave it to cool, allowing the juice to sink into the sponge. The surface should have a lovely crystalline sheen. Cut into whatever size or shape you fancy.

These fanciful little cakes were originally intended to take on a picnic – a bag still warm from the oven would be welcome on any journey. Bake them as close to the time of eating as possible, a couple of hours in advance won't hurt, but the warmer they are the more meltingly tender they are likely to be.

Madeleines traditionally are baked in a special tray to give small scallop-shaped cakes which are fluted on the underside. But these can be baked in any small cake tins, such as fairy-cake racks.

date madeleines

90ml water

110g pitted dates, chopped

$^1/_2$ teaspoon bicarbonate of soda

2 large eggs

25g vanilla or caster sugar

Finely grated zest of 1 lemon

2 tablespoons clear honey

50g self-raising flour

$^1/_2$ teaspoon baking powder

Pinch of salt

50g ground almonds

110g unsalted butter, melted,
    plus 10g for greasing

Icing sugar for dusting

Makes 15–20

Bring the water and dates to the boil in a small saucepan and simmer for 4 minutes until the dates turn quite mushy, then stir in the bicarbonate of soda. Whisk the eggs and sugar together until they are almost white, then add the lemon zest and honey. Sift the flour and baking powder together and lightly fold it into the egg mixture, then add the salt and the ground almonds, taking care not to overwork. Gently fold in the cooled, melted butter and the dates and their water and chill the mixture for 30 minutes.

Preheat the oven to 190°C fan/210°C/gas mark 6$^1/_2$. Brush the insides of a madeleine tray or one or two fairy-cake racks with a little melted butter. Spoon the mixture into the prepared moulds, filling each one two-thirds full. Bake the madeleines in the oven for 8–10 minutes or until golden. Run a knife round the edge of the cakes, turn them out onto a wire rack and dust the tops with icing sugar.

While this may seem like a lot of oil, it replaces butter, and actually works out less per square than you would use to dress a portion of green salad. And with all those eggs, fruit and almonds, it's not an unhealthy option. As well as making a teatime treat, serve this as pudding with a dollop of crème fraîche or scoop of ice-cream.

raspberry and almond traybake

225g ground almonds
30g flaked almonds
280g golden caster sugar
2 teaspoons baking powder, sifted
60g fresh white breadcrumbs
6 large eggs
300ml sunflower or groundnut oil
Finely grated zest of 2 oranges
125g raspberries

Makes 1 x 30 x 23cm traybake

Preheat the oven to 190°C fan/210–220°C/gas mark 6½. Mix together the ground and flaked almonds, 180g caster sugar, baking powder and breadcrumbs in a large bowl. Beat in the eggs thoroughly using a wooden spoon, then the oil, and stir in the orange zest. Transfer the mixture to a greased 30 x 23 x 4cm baking tin and smooth the surface. Scatter over the raspberries, then the remaining sugar, and bake for 25–30 minutes or until the cake is golden and a skewer inserted into the centre comes out clean. Run a knife around the edge of the cake and leave it to cool before cutting into squares or slices.

Jammy dodgers are such a great idea, but I find commercial ones just too sweet and gloopy. The cut-out in the centre here could be any shape – hearts have real child appeal. Offer these with some chocolate-dipped marshmallows for instant playground cred.

jammy dodgers

Biscuits

225g unsalted butter, diced
100g caster sugar
200g plain flour
115g ground almonds
150g raspberry jam
Icing sugar for dusting

Chocolate marshmallows

60g dark chocolate (50% cocoa solids),
   broken up
200g pink and white marshmallows

Makes approx. 30 of each

Place the butter, sugar, flour and ground almonds in a food processor and process to a dough. Wrap the dough in clingfilm and rest in the fridge overnight.

Preheat the oven to 140°C fan/160°C/gas mark 3. Knead the dough until pliable then, working with half at a time, thinly roll it out on a lightly floured worktop and cut out biscuits with a 5cm fluted round cutter. The dough can be rolled twice. Using a palette knife, transfer the biscuits to baking sheets, then cut out hearts or some other shape from the centre of just over half of them (to allow for breakages once they are cooked) using a miniature cutter about 2cm in diameter. Bake the biscuits (including the cut-outs) for 30 minutes until pale gold then remove them and leave to cool. Depending on the size of your oven and how many baking trays you have, you may need to cook the biscuits in two batches, in which case store the second batch on a plate in the fridge while the first one is baking.

Work the jam in a bowl with a spoon until it's smooth. Dust the cut-out biscuits and shapes you removed with icing sugar. Using the palette knife, spread a little jam into the centre of each plain biscuit and sandwich with one of the cut-out biscuits so the jam shows through the hole. The remaining miniature shapes can be sandwiched together with a good-quality chocolate spread.

For the chocolate marshmallows, place the chocolate in a bowl set over a pan with a little simmering water in it, and gently melt, stirring. Dip the top of each marshmallow into the chocolate, then place, chocolate end up, on a plate to set for 1 hour. Skewer the marshmallows with cocktail sticks through the uncoated base, and arrange on a plate.

I judge all macaroons by those I once ate for breakfast at Maison du Chocolat in Paris, with tiny cups of the richest hot chocolate. These macaroons are soft and fudgey, and as well as being delicious eaten for tea they make a good after-dinner treat.

pink macaroons with dark chocolate

125g ground almonds

125g icing sugar, sifted

1 large egg white

50ml crème fraîche

1/2 teaspoon vanilla extract

Pink food colouring, paste or liquid

75g dark chocolate (approx. 70% cocoa solids), broken up

Cocoa powder for dusting

Makes 12

Preheat the oven to 200°C fan/220°C/gas mark 7. Place the ground almonds, icing sugar and egg white in a food processor and blend together for 1–2 minutes. Add the crème fraîche a teaspoon at a time, then the vanilla extract and a little food colouring. Dab a little of the mixture onto four corners of a large baking sheet and line it with baking paper. Drop three-quarter teaspoons of the mixture in domes spaced 2cm apart, staggering the rows. Leave the macaroons to stand for 10–15 minutes.

Bake the macaroons for 8–11 minutes, propping the door open with a wooden spoon, until they start to colour. Turn the tray round 4 minutes into baking to ensure they cook evenly.

The baker's trick to removing the macaroons from the paper is to run a little cold water between the baking paper and the tray. You may need to do this on two or three sides of the paper until the whole sheet is wet. Leave the macaroons to cool; they should then be quite easy to remove from the damp paper.

Put the chocolate in a bowl set over a saucepan of simmering water and gently melt it. Spread 1/2 teaspoon onto one macaroon, sandwich with another and place on a rack. Repeat with all the macaroons. Once the chocolate has set, dust them on both sides with cocoa and pile onto a plate. They will keep in an airtight container for several days.

This is a thick, cakey shortbread set with dried cherries and drizzled with a thread of rosewater icing. Dried cranberries, which are equally piquant, can be used too.

iced cherry shortbread

Shortbread
350g unsalted butter, diced
175g golden caster sugar
275g plain flour
200g ground almonds
Finely grated zest of 1 orange
$1/2$ teaspoon sea salt
100g dried cherries

Icing
75g icing sugar, sifted
$3/4$ tablespoon rosewater
Pink food colouring, paste
  or liquid (optional)

Makes approx. 30

Unless you have a large food processor, you will need to make the dough in two batches. Place all the ingredients for the shortbread except the dried fruit in a food processor and reduce to crumbs, stopping the motor as these start to cling together in lumps. Transfer the mixture to a bowl. Fold in the cherries. Using your hands bring the shortbread together into a dough. Press it into the base of a 30 x 23 x 4cm non-stick baking tin, laying a sheet of clingfilm over the top and smoothing it with your fingers. Cover the surface of the tin with extra clingfilm and chill for 1 hour.

Preheat the oven to 140°C fan/160°C/gas mark 3. Remove the clingfilm and prick the shortbread all over with a fork and bake for 45 minutes until lightly coloured. Run a knife around the edge and leave it to cool.

Blend the icing sugar with the rosewater in a bowl and, if you like, tint it a pale pink with a little food colouring. Using a teaspoon, drizzle the icing in a thin stream over the cake and leave it for about 1 hour to set. Cut into 3cm squares.

This has always been a personal weakness, a panacea in times of trouble, I'll drive several miles out of my way to find a bakery with aptly named Paradise Slices on the shelf. It's the combination of cake and pastry that does it, the same magic as a bakewell tart. Here I've spread a shortbread base with raspberry jam and baked a coconut sponge set with sultanas on top. But nothing I say is going to do them justice – you'll just have to bake some.

paradise slice

Shortbread

175g unsalted butter
75g golden caster sugar
150g plain flour
100g ground almonds
Finely grated zest of 1 orange or lemon
(optional)

Filling

120g raspberry jam

Sponge

110g unsalted butter, diced
150g golden caster sugar
4 medium eggs
150g desiccated coconut
75g ground almonds
1 teaspoon baking powder, sifted
110g sultanas
Icing sugar for dusting

Makes approx. 16

Put all the ingredients for the shortbread in a food processor and reduce to crumbs, then keep the motor running until the mixture comes together into a ball. It will be very soft and sticky at this point. Press it into the base of a 30 x 23 x 4cm non-stick baking tin, laying a sheet of clingfilm over the top and smoothing it with your fingers. Cover the surface of the tin with extra clingfilm and chill for 1 hour.

Preheat the oven to 140°C fan/160°C/gas mark 3. Remove the clingfilm, prick the shortbread with a fork and bake for 25–30 minutes until just beginning to colour. Leave to cool.

Increase the oven temperature to 170°C fan/190°C/gas mark 5. Work the jam with a spoon in a bowl until it is smooth, then spread it in a thin layer over the shortbread base using a palette knife. Put the butter and sugar in a food processor and cream together, then incorporate the eggs. Pour the mixture into a bowl and fold in the coconut, ground almonds, baking powder and sultanas. Smooth the mixture on top of the jam and bake for 25–30 minutes until the sponge has set and the top is golden. Run a knife around the edge of the cake and leave it to cool. Cut it in half lengthways, then across into 2cm slices. Dust with icing sugar and transfer to a serving plate.

plum muffins

225g plain flour

2 teaspoons baking powder

75g golden caster sugar

1/2 teaspoon sea salt

1 medium egg

200ml milk

30g unsalted butter, melted

4 red or purple plums (approx. 180g), stoned and diced

Finely grated zest of 1 lemon

75g macadamias, coarsely chopped

Pink writing icing

Makes 10

Preheat the oven to 180°C fan/200°C/gas mark 6. Combine the flour, baking powder, sugar and salt in a large bowl. Whisk the egg in another bowl, then whisk in the milk and butter. Pour this over the dry ingredients and stir until just mixed, you needn't be too thorough about this, then fold in the plums and lemon zest.

Set about 10 paper muffin cases into a muffin-tin rack. Spoon the mixture into the cases so they are half full, scatter over the nuts and bake for 17–20 minutes until risen and lightly coloured. Transfer the muffins to a rack and leave to cool to room temperature, then decorate them with a zigzag of pink icing. Muffins are at their best and fluffiest the day they are made.

gorgeous cakes

Even those who eschew yeast cookery and making bread are happy enough to knock out a batch of scones. I can think of little more enjoyable than a lazy tea on the lawn with a plate of buttered scones, hot and crusty from the oven, with strawberry jam.

scones with strawberry jam

500g plain flour

75g icing sugar

25g baking power

1/2 teaspoon sea salt

125g unsalted butter, chilled and diced, plus extra to serve

2 medium eggs

Milk

Strawberry jam to serve

Makes 7–8

Preheat the oven to 180°C fan/200°C/gas mark 6. Sift the flour, icing sugar and baking powder into a large bowl or food processor and add the salt. Rub in the butter, add the eggs and enough milk to bring the dough together. Roll the dough out 2cm thick on a floured surface and cut out 7 or 8 scones using a round 7cm cutter. Leave these to rest on a baking tray for 20 minutes then brush the tops with milk and bake for 17–20 minutes. They are most delicious eaten warm, slit and spread with butter and strawberry jam, but also good at room temperature.

We all need a foolproof recipe for pancakes at our fingertips: teatime for children is turned into a feast. I know few who aren't passionate about them; once a year just isn't enough. Most children adore a sprinkling of caster sugar and squeeze of lemon. A little chocolate powder also goes down well, as does a drizzle of maple syrup, or raspberry jam. And ice-cream for a real treat.

perfect pancakes

250g plain flour
Golden caster sugar
Pinch of sea salt
3 large eggs and 2 egg yolks
600ml full-fat milk
40g unsalted butter, melted

Makes approx. 16

To prepare the pancakes by hand, place the flour, sugar (1 tablespoon for sweet and a pinch for savoury) and salt in a large bowl, add the eggs and yolks and mix to a lumpy wet paste using a spoon. Whisk in the milk, a little to begin with to smooth out the lumps, then in bolder streams once you have a creamy batter. Alternatively, place all the ingredients except for the butter in a blender and whizz until smooth. Give the sides and bottom of the blender a stir to make sure there's no flour clinging, and whizz again. Leave the batter to stand for at least 30 minutes, then stir in the melted butter, transferring the batter to a bowl if you made it in a blender.

Heat 1 or 2 non-stick frying pans with an 18cm base over a medium-high heat for several minutes. For children you might want to use a slightly smaller pan. Ladle in just enough batter to coat the base, tipping it to allow it to run evenly over the surface. If the pan is hot enough, the batter will sizzle as soon as it hits the base. Cook for 30 seconds until the top side appears dry and lacey at the edges and it is golden and lacey underneath. Loosen the edges using a palette knife or spatula (non-stick for a non-stick pan), slip this underneath and flip it over. Cook it for 30 seconds and then slip it onto a plate. I always discard the first one; for no explicable reason it never seems to work properly. Cook the remainder likewise and either dish them up as soon as they are cooked, or pile up on a plate and cover with foil to keep warm.

You can also make them in advance, cover and chill them once they are cool, and reheat them briefly on each side in a dry frying pan. In this case they keep well for several days. Serve them rolled or folded – I come down in favour of the latter, in French tradition cradled in a napkin, to save burnt fingers.

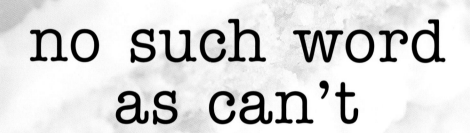

no such word
as can't

Why do you say no to cakes? If it's because of food intolerance – no nuts, no wheat for you – then you should check each cake's ingredients list to make sure there's nothing on it that hates you personally. But if it's because most cakes are too sweet or rich for you – not your calorie intake, your actual tastes – you should welcome this chapter too. It isn't about poor substitutes, it isn't about making do with less. Many of these alternative cakes are based on ground nuts rather than flour, which makes for a looser, moister luxurious sponge. (One of my all-time favourite sponge recipes is blended of ground nuts, eggs and sugar, so there isn't any butter in it at all.)

A frosting or filling doesn't need butter or cream to achieve a rich smooth texture: I've used low-fat cheeses such as cream cheese, fromage blanc or ricotta (despite its velvety nature, it's as low in fat as cottage cheese). To kick off, there's a version of Claudia Roden's classic Orange and Almond cake – made of just that, plus eggs – mother-cake to all alternative dessert recipes. Mine has figs in it for an even more Mediterranean feel. Enjoy. Without fear or guilt.

I have always loved Claudia Roden's Orange and Almond cake. It's one that without employing any fat is supremely moist and scented. This take on it is decorated with figs, and a campari glaze that offsets the fruit.

fig and orange cake with campari glaze

2 medium oranges
6 medium eggs
225g ground almonds
225g golden caster sugar
1 teaspoon baking powder, sifted
3 figs, stalks cut off
100g redcurrant jelly
1 tablespoon campari

Makes 1 x 20cm cake

Place the oranges in a medium saucepan and three-quarters cover them with water. Bring to the boil, cover and simmer for 2 hours, checking the water level towards the end to make sure they don't boil dry. Leave them to cool, then remove them from the pan, quarter and pick out any seeds, and the hard core where the stalk was attached. Place the oranges in a food processor and reduce to a purée.

Preheat the oven to 170°C fan/190°C/gas mark 5 and butter a 20cm cake tin 9cm deep with a removable base. Whisk the eggs in a large bowl, then fold in the ground almonds, sugar, baking powder and the orange purée. Transfer the mixture to the prepared tin and smooth the surface. Thickly slice the figs (and eat the ends), decorate the surface of the cake so you have a ring of fig slices around the outside and one in the centre. Bake for 55–60 minutes or until the surface is a deep gold and a skewer inserted into the centre comes out with just a few moist crumbs clinging. Run a knife around the edge and leave it to cool.

To glaze the cake, heat the redcurrant jelly with the campari in a small saucepan, smoothing it with a spoon, and simmer for 1 minute. Pass the glaze through a sieve and use it to generously coat the top and sides of the cake, using a pastry brush. Leave to set for 1 hour.

Perhaps the hardest ingredient of all to omit from a cake is eggs, and this cake is a pleasant surprise – it would be hard to guess their absence.

sour cherry yogurt cake

Cake

75g pine nuts

150g dried sour cherries, plus 1 tablespoon

100g unsalted butter

100g golden caster sugar

300g natural yogurt

1 teaspoon vanilla extract

250g plain flour

2 teaspoons bicarbonate of soda

Icing

100g icing sugar, sifted, plus a little extra

1 tablespoon (approx.) fresh orange juice, sieved

Pink food colouring liquid (optional)

Makes 1 x 22cm loaf

Preheat the oven to 160°C fan/180°C/gas mark 4 and butter a 22cm (1.3l) loaf tin. Put the pine nuts in a food processor, reduce them to a paste then transfer to a bowl. Finely chop the 150g dried cherries, and add these to the paste. Cream the butter and sugar in the processor, then add the yogurt and vanilla. Sift the dry ingredients together and add to the mixture in two goes, then transfer it to a large bowl and thoroughly fold in the cherries and pine nut paste. Spoon the cake mixture into the prepared loaf tin, level the surface and bake for 50 minutes or until risen and golden, and a skewer inserted into the centre comes out clean. Run a knife around the edge and leave to cool.

Turn the cake out onto a board to ice it. Blend the 100g icing sugar and orange juice in a bowl, add a couple of drops of pink food colouring, if you like, and drizzle down the centre of the cake, smoothing it towards the sides using a palette knife. Don't worry about completely covering the surface, or about it trickling down the sides. Decorate the surface with the extra dried cherries, then dust over a little icing sugar using a tea strainer. Leave to set for 1 hour.

We're all familiar with carrot cake, healthier than many in that it relies on vegetable oil rather than butter, and contains carrots and nuts. Beetroot is just as good, with the bonus of colouring the cake a pretty speckled pink.

pink speckled cake

Cake

150g raw beetroot, grated

200ml groundnut oil

250g golden caster sugar

3 medium eggs, separated

3 tablespoons milk

100g hazelnuts, roasted and chopped

200g plain flour

2 teaspoons baking powder

$1/2$ teaspoon each ground ginger,
  cinnamon and nutmeg

Frosting

180g unsalted butter, softened

150g icing sugar, sifted

450g low-fat cream or curd cheese

1 teaspoon vanilla extract

Pink and pale blue sugar flowers
  to decorate

Makes 1 x 20cm cake

Preheat the oven to 170°C fan/190°C/gas mark 5 and butter two 20cm cake tins 9cm deep with a removable base. Line the base with baking paper and butter this too. Place about 1 teaspoon of the grated beetroot in a small bowl, cover it with 2 teaspoons boiling water and set aside (this is to colour the frosting later on).

Whisk the oil and caster sugar in a large bowl, then whisk in the egg yolks and milk, and fold in the remaining beetroot and nuts. Sift the flour and baking powder together and stir this into the mixture, and then the spices. Whisk the egg whites in another bowl until they are stiff, and fold them in three goes into the cake mixture. Divide this between the tins, smoothing the surface and bake for 30–35 minutes or until shrinking from the sides and a skewer inserted into the centre comes out clean. Run a knife around the edge of the cakes and leave them to cool.

To make the frosting, cream the butter and icing sugar in a food processor. Remove the butter icing to a bowl, blend with the cream cheese until smooth, and work in the vanilla extract and a couple of teaspoons of the beetroot liquor to tint it a pale pink.

Turn the cakes onto a board and remove the baking paper. Spread about a quarter of the frosting over the top of one of the cakes, sandwich with the other and use the remaining frosting to coat the top and sides. Decorate the top and sides with sugar flowers and place in the fridge to set for about 1 hour. If not serving straight away then cover with clingfilm and chill, and remove from the fridge about 30 minutes before eating.

As lavish as the most extravagant cream cake and worthy of the title gâteau, this cake is virtually fat-free. It keeps well in the fridge for several days, as the liquid in the ricotta seeps down into the sponge and keeps it moist.

raspberry ricotta cake

Ricotta cream

3 tablespoons seedless raspberry jam
2 x 250g tubs of ricotta, drained
   of any liquid

Sponge

225g hazelnuts, shelled and blanched
4 medium eggs, separated
150g golden caster sugar
1 teaspoon baking powder, sifted

200g raspberries
Icing sugar for dusting

Makes 1 x 20cm cake

To make the ricotta cream, whizz the jam in a food processor until smooth, then add the ricotta and whizz again (if you do this by hand the ricotta will remain grainy). Transfer it to a bowl, cover and chill for several hours, during which time it will firm up a little.

Preheat the oven to 180°C fan/200°C/gas mark 6 and butter two 20cm shallow sandwich or deep cake tins with a removable base. Grind the hazelnuts to a powder in a coffee grinder – you will need to do this in batches. Stiffly whisk the egg whites in a medium bowl. In a separate large bowl whisk together the egg yolks and sugar until pale and creamy. Fold the egg whites into the egg and sugar mixture in three goes, then fold in the ground hazelnuts and baking powder. Divide the cake mixture between the two prepared tins, smooth the surface and bake them for 20 minutes until the sponge has begun to shrink from the sides. Run a knife around the edge of the cakes and leave them to cool in the tin.

Remove the collars from the cakes, but you can leave one on the base for ease of serving. Spread half the ricotta cream over this layer to within 2cm of the edge, then sandwich with the other half, gently pressing it down until the cream approaches the edge. Spread the remaining cream on the surface, this time taking it up to the edge, and decorate with the raspberries. Dust them with icing sugar and set aside in a cool place. If keeping the cake longer than a few hours, cover, chill and bring it back up to room temperature for 30–60 minutes before serving.

You only have to peruse the ingredients of this yummy cake to work out how good for you it is. The recipe derives from a favourite organic gastro-pub that's local to me – the Pelican in Notting Hill – named after its creator, Tasha. I'm sure other dried fruits would work beautifully too, though it's worth checking the small print on the back of the pack: I'm disappointed by how many 'new' dried fruits on the market like papaya, sour cherries and pineapple contain added sugar.

tasha's apricot and hazelnut cake

Cake

225g ready-to-eat dried apricots
1 x 7cm cinnamon stick
5 cloves
5 green cardamom pods
Finely grated zest and juice of 2 lemons
6 medium eggs, separated
125g golden caster sugar
50g light muscovado sugar
125g hazelnuts, skinned
Icing sugar for dusting

Cinnamon yogurt

200g crème fraîche
200g Greek yogurt
1/4 teaspoon ground cinnamon
2 tablespoons honey, preferably Greek

Makes 1 x 23cm cake

Put the apricots, spices, lemon zest and juice and 150ml water in a small saucepan. Bring to the boil, then simmer over a low heat for 20–30 minutes until the apricots are tender and have absorbed all the liquid. Watch carefully towards the end to make sure they don't catch. Remove the spices and purée the apricots in a food processor. Transfer to a bowl and leave to cool.

Preheat the oven to 160°C fan/180°C/gas mark 4 and butter a 23cm cake tin 6cm deep with a removable base. Place the egg yolks and sugars in the food processor (there's no need to wash the bowl out after the apricots) and whizz until pale and creamy. Grind the hazelnuts in a coffee grinder, you will need to do this in batches, and incorporate them into the egg and sugar mixture. Work in the puréed apricots, and transfer to a large bowl. Whisk the egg whites in another bowl until they are stiff, then fold them into the mixture in three goes. Spoon this into the prepared tin and smooth the surface. Bake for 50 minutes or until golden and a skewer inserted into the centre comes out clean. Run a knife around the edge of the cake and leave it to cool.

Blend all the ingredients for the cinnamon yogurt in a bowl. Cover with clingfilm and chill until required. Dust the cake with icing sugar and serve in slices, accompanied with cinnamon yogurt if it's for pud.

All meringues are wheat-free and low in fat (we'll gloss over the sugar). This version will also cater for anyone who can't take cow's milk, and the goat's cheese filling perfectly offsets the sweetness.

raspberry goat's cheese meringues

3 large egg whites
180g caster sugar
Pink food colouring liquid (optional)
50g (approx.) raspberry jam
100g soft goat's cheese

Makes approx. 12 sandwiched meringues

Preheat the oven to 120°C fan/140°C/gas mark 1. Place the egg whites in a large bowl and whisk them until they rise into a froth the consistency of shaving foam. Sprinkle over 1 heaped tablespoon of sugar at a time, whisking well with each addition, until you have a smooth, glossy meringue. You can increase the sugar to 2 tablespoons towards the end. In theory the meringue should be stiff enough for you to hold the bowl upside-down above your head. If you wish, colour the mixture pink with a few drops of food colouring.

Line one or two baking trays with baking paper, using a little of the meringue mixture to stick down the corners. Drop $1/2$ tablespoons of the mixture onto the paper, leaving plenty of space between each meringue. Place the meringues in the oven and cook for $1^1/2$–2 hours (if you are using two trays switch them around halfway through). After this time the meringues should be crisp on the outside, and if you tap the base it should sound hollow within. Remove and leave them to cool. They can be stored in an airtight container for 2 weeks.

Shortly before serving, spread half the meringues with the jam, and the other half with the goat's cheese, and sandwich together. Cover and chill if not serving within the hour. They should keep well for a few hours, in which case bring them back up to room temperature for 30 minutes before serving.

index